MW00881128

Growing Andrea

SPECIAL NEEDS, SPECIAL GRACE

Hannah Hartley

WESTBOW
PRESS®
A DIVISION OF THOMAS NELSON
& ZONDERVAN

Copyright © 2021 Hannah Hartley.

All rights reserved. No part of this book may be used or reproduced by any means, graphic, electronic, or mechanical, including photocopying, recording, taping or by any information storage retrieval system without the written permission of the author except in the case of brief quotations embodied in critical articles and reviews.

This book is a work of non-fiction. Unless otherwise noted, the author and the publisher make no explicit guarantees as to the accuracy of the information contained in this book and in some cases, names of people and places have been altered to protect their privacy.

WestBow Press books may be ordered through booksellers or by contacting:

WestBow Press
A Division of Thomas Nelson & Zondervan
1663 Liberty Drive
Bloomington, IN 47403
www.westbowpress.com
844-714-3454

Because of the dynamic nature of the Internet, any web addresses or links contained in this book may have changed since publication and may no longer be valid. The views expressed in this work are solely those of the author and do not necessarily reflect the views of the publisher, and the publisher hereby disclaims any responsibility for them.

Any people depicted in stock imagery provided by Getty Images are models, and such images are being used for illustrative purposes only. Certain stock imagery © Getty Images.

ISBN: 978-1-6642-3969-2 (sc)
ISBN: 978-1-6642-3971-5 (hc)
ISBN: 978-1-6642-3970-8 (e)

Library of Congress Control Number: 2021913688

Print information available on the last page.

WestBow Press rev. date: 07/22/2021

Scripture quotations marked NIV are taken from The Holy Bible, New International Version®, NIV® Copyright © 1973, 1978, 1984, 2011 by Biblica, Inc.® Used by permission. All rights reserved worldwide.

Scripture quotations marked NASB are taken from The New American Standard Bible®, Copyright © 1960, 1962, 1963, 1968, 1971, 1972, 1973, 1975, 1977, 1995 by The Lockman Foundation. Used by permission.

Scripture quotations marked NLT are taken from the Holy Bible, New Living Translation, Copyright © 1996, 2004, 2015 by Tyndale House Foundation. Used by permission of Tyndale House Publishers, Inc., Carol Stream, Illinois 60188. All rights reserved.

Scripture quotations marked ESV taken from The Holy Bible, English Standard Version® (ESV®), Copyright © 2001 by Crossway, a publishing ministry of Good News Publishers. All rights reserved.

Scripture quotations marked NKJV are taken from the New King James Version®. Copyright © 1982 by Thomas Nelson. Used by permission. All rights reserved.

CONTENTS

INTRODUCTION

Hang on tight and get ready for the wildest,
saddest, happiest, most challenging and
most rewarding ride of your life!
—Sylvia Phillips

It is to parents raising a child who is different and to the
ones who seek to understand those children that I dedicate
this book. Whether this means Down syndrome, cerebral
palsy, autism, developmental delays, or a child who simply
marches to their own drummer, the path goes in much the
same direction. As their parents, we cry, rejoice, worry,
and work tirelessly. We're relentless, determined, and
protective. We feel lost at times, confused, and alone and
suffer with broken hearts each time the world rejects our
child. We are convinced this child has a divine destiny and
purpose, and we will stop at nothing to assure they are on
the path that will lead them to discover it.

We have been given a unique opportunity to impact the
world. Remember as you travel this road that you are not
alone. We are on this ride together. Let's help each other

avoid the potholes and get around the unexpected curves. And if we can't, then let's at least hold hands and do this together. This child is God's gift to you, and God Himself is with you every step of the way. There is a plan of greatness and purpose already in place for your child. God will bring it to pass. Trust Him. Lean into His comforting arms when you feel lost and alone. Seek His wisdom when you are trying to make the right decision. Commit your child's life to Him daily. Then co-labor with God to bring about His will.

You and your beautiful child are embarking on a once-in-a-lifetime journey that can and will change the world.

*But Mary treasured up all these things
and pondered them in her heart.*
—Luke 2:19 (NIV)

ONE

ༀ

Soil

Sow with a view to righteousness, reap in
accordance with kindness; break up your
fallow ground, for it is time to seek the Lord
until He comes to rain righteousness on you.
—Hosea 10:12 (NASB)

What does it mean to "break up your fallow ground?" I looked up the word *fallow* (Oxford Dictionary on Lexico.com) and discovered it is an adjective meaning "plowed and harrowed but left unsown for a period in order to restore its fertility."

Have you noticed that when God is about to do a great thing for you, He first prepares you? He never springs something on us that He has not first prepared us for, although I admit it sometimes feels like He hasn't. But if

1

you pause and look back, I am certain you will see how He was working. He was breaking up your fallow ground.

The desire to be a mom began in me before an age I can even remember. All I ever wanted to be was a mommy. Parents and teachers would encourage me to have a career goal, as "mommy" was no career. So to appease them, I said, "Okay, I want to be a teacher." But God knew in my heart of hearts being a mommy was the only true passion I really had.

The seed of faith began in me at about the same time. My dad used to call God "My Partner." Throughout childhood, he would make it clear that God was in everything. A rainbow would appear, and he would say, "There's my Partner's handiwork." Or a parking spot would become available at a busy mall, and he would say with his thumb up and a nod toward heaven, "Ah, thanks, Partner." The rain would stop just in time for an event, and my dad would acknowledge aloud that this was his Partner at work.

My dad guarded his quiet time with his Partner, which was at sunset every single day of his life. Sunsets were my dad's delight! Time with God was my dad's priority. Even if we had company, he would excuse himself and leave for this consecrated time. My parents eventually moved to Palomar Mountain, and my dad had a viewpoint there of the land below all the way to the Pacific Ocean. Each season of the year, you could find him there at sunset, even in the snow. This was his sanctuary. This was his time to chat with his Partner. Even his friends and the residents of Palomar Mountain knew not to disturb him and would just pass by if they saw him at the lookout. They knew. This was his holy place, his time of prayer and thanksgiving, not a time to chitchat with friends and socialize.

Dad was not your conventional Christian. He would bring his bottle of Coors Light with him, lean on the hood of his truck, and commune with his Partner. But he relied on Him daily and never missed his appointment. He never quoted scripture, yet he instilled in me through his actions that "apart from me you can do nothing" (John 15:5 NIV).

My mother was:

- A lady in every way
- Versatile when life threw a curve
- Artistic and talented
- Caring and loving
- Tenderhearted and forgiving
- Humble and kind
- The rock of our family

But it wasn't until she was gone—and I had watched her die as beautifully as she had lived—that I truly realized how much this family needed her and learned from her. She was my dad's strength and the glue of our family. When she died after fifty-two years of marriage, my dad was never the same again.

My dad, a retired senior chief in the navy, was six feet two inches tall and always walked with pride and perfect posture. As we left my mom's funeral, I saw him slump for the first time in my life. And for the next eight years, until his death, I watched him slowly disintegrate from grief and Alzheimer's disease.

I did well in school, and my parents were so excited when I graduated early and started college. But after one year, I left school to marry my high school sweetheart and follow him around the country on his navy transfers. It was a great adventure, and although I was young, my heart continued to long for a baby.

Month after month and year after year we tried. Fertility tests proved he was fine; it was me. I only ovulated twice a year, which of course significantly reduced my odds of getting pregnant. I spent years in the Word on my knees, claiming His promises, waiting, hoping, and believing. But month after month resulted in complete devastation. At times it felt like experiencing the grief of death over and over. For those of you who have struggled or are struggling with infertility, my heart goes out to you. I know how difficult this season is. But have faith. God is at work in you and preparing you for His next great blessing.

During this same time, I witnessed several friends elect to have abortions. I cried out to God, "Why? You promise to give us the desires of our hearts, yet You are giving babies to people willing to dispose of them. Why?"

But it seemed that my prayers were going nowhere. I knew not to question God or His ways. I knew I was supposed to stay in peace, rest in Him, and trust that His ways are not our ways. I confess I could not do that. So in a way I raged at God, "You're a *just* God? This doesn't look like justice to me!" I was a spoiled child demanding my own way and making my defense to God with only a dim understanding of the scriptures I was quoting back to Him.

It had been seven years since we first began trying to get pregnant, seven long and painful years, years that tested my devotion to God, years that caused me to question His goodness, years that stretched me beyond any emotional limits I could have previously imagined. But at the end of that time, I was able to honestly pray, "Lord, I surrender."

Why it took so long to get me to that place, God only knows. But what I do know is that seven is one of the most significant numbers of the Bible. It is the number of spiritual perfection. It is the number stamped on every work of God. God created the heavens and the earth and rested on day seven. There are seven spirits of God: the Spirit of the Lord and the Spirits of wisdom, understanding, counsel, might, knowledge, and fear of the Lord (Isaiah 11:2–3). In the book of Revelation, seven lampstands represent the seven churches of Asia. There are seven seals and seven angels of the seven churches. Revelation speaks of seven stars, seven crowns, seven bowls, seven thunders, and so on.

Consider that there are even seven colors in a rainbow. I am no theologian by any means, but consider this: The number 7 is used 735 times in the Bible. And if we include the words "sevenfold" and "seventh," our total jumps to 860 references. Surely this is an important number to

God, and it is the number of years he spent patiently and diligently working on me, working on my heart.

It could not have been easy for Him to listen to me crying out all that time. It could not have been enjoyable for Him to watch His beloved daughter suffering through so much pain and heartache. But in the end, it must have been worth it for Him to hear me say and to truly mean with all my heart those two little words, those two powerful words, "I surrender."

I told God, "If I am never to become a mother, I am ready to accept that. Please tell me what to do, and I will do it with all my heart."

I ordered college catalogs and prepared to go back to school and become something. I didn't know what but knew I had to start building a future without children of my own. I was truly trusting God to lead me now, and I was willing to follow … finally.

TWO

ૐ

Seed

For you created my inmost being; you knit me together in my mother's womb. I praise you because I am fearfully and wonderfully made; your works are wonderful; I know that full well.

—Psalm 139:13–14 (NIV)

wo months after sincerely giving God control, I became terribly ill. I went to the doctor for what I thought was a bad cough and cold. The exam and x-rays resulted in a diagnosis of pneumonia. Multiple x-rays were taken, and I was prescribed tetracycline, an antibiotic, and cough medicine with codeine, among other medications. After two weeks, I returned to the doctor to tell him I was not getting better and, in fact, was so tired

I could barely stay awake. I asked if he could prescribe something else. He ordered a urine test.

The results of the urine test showed I was pregnant. That moment was like one you see in movies. All images blurred, and sounds were muffled except for the words, "You are pregnant." The doctor proceeded to say that I might miscarry as the medications I had taken were not compatible with pregnancy and would be harmful to the fetus. He suggested I should not get too excited. What? Don't get too excited? *How is that even possible?* I wondered.

I drove home so elated that I bet there was a glow coming from my car. I walked in, literally fell to my knees, and cried my thanks, praise, and joy to God for this miracle!

My follow-up appointment was with an OB the next week. He examined me, reviewed my chart, and coldly said, "Yes, I can confirm that you are pregnant, but I highly advise that you abort this baby. It has been exposed to far too many teratogens, and the baby will quite likely be damaged and grossly deformed."

It has been over forty-one years since I heard those words, yet I remember each one exactly. My response was a question. I asked him, "If you had been trying to have a baby for seven years and finally were given this one, what would you do?"

Again, he was cold and absolute in his response, "I would most definitely abort." The doctor went on to say that after the first pregnancy, the body *learns* what to do, and subsequent pregnancies occur more easily. But subsequent pregnancies will not be this baby. What about *this* baby? I told him that I would not have an abortion and left his office.

When I got to my car, I cried. It was a very brief sadness followed by a total acceptance of what might be, but my joy quickly returned and remained with me throughout my pregnancy. As soon as I arrived home from this appointment, I randomly opened my Bible and read these words, "With man, this is impossible, but with God, all things are possible" (Matthew 19:26 NIV).

I claimed that verse for the remainder of my pregnancy and literally had no concern for my baby's well-being or the outcome. I was not in denial. I had heard the doctor. But God had also prepared me for this in the preceding years, and I happily accepted any outcome He had planned. I *knew* this baby was a gift and the result of answered prayer.

I walked around for the next seven and a half months like I was the only pregnant woman there has ever been. I was so happy, so full of joy, so content. God had truly prepared the soil of my heart, and grossly deformed or not, I was determined to give this baby the best of me.

My pregnancy proceeded better than normal. I had no morning sickness, no aches and pains, and no cravings. I had joy. I felt better physically, emotionally, and spiritually than at any other time in my life. At the time, I had a friend who was also pregnant, and her baby was born a day after mine. Throughout our pregnancies, we would compare notes. Her baby moved constantly; you could see her baby moving under her clothes. I was a little envious, as Andrea barely moved and would go days, apparently asleep. But I thought I just had a mellow little baby and that hers would be more active. That's fine.

Andrea was born full term in 1979 at a healthy seven and a half pounds. She was breech and delivered by c-section. Her little legs were drawn up by her body in the shape of the letter "M" because of her position in the birth canal. She was the most beautiful newborn ever to grace the planet (as seen through mommy-vision). She had all her fingers, toes, arms, legs, eyes, nose, mouth, and ears. She had it all. There were no deformities and no flaws. I kept the same OB doctor for delivery who had told me to abort her.

He never even congratulated me. He simply said, "It's a girl."

No matter, I prayed he would learn from this and hopefully not be so quick to advise abortion to his next patient in similar circumstances.

You know the love of your firstborn child, of any child. I never wanted to put her down. I even had a nurse tell me, "You're going to spoil that baby." I was? Didn't you know that was the plan?

Struggle to Sprout

"My grace is sufficient for you, for my power
is made perfect in weakness."
                    —2 Corinthians 12:9 (NIV)

I believe there is power in a name or, at the very least, some self-fulfilling prophecy, so we chose the name Andrea, which means brave. I felt that if she should come into the world disabled, she would need this attribute. The first moment I held her, I knew something was not right. She was weak and floppy. I had to scoop her up with both my arms; otherwise her arms and legs would flop and dangle downward. I have always loved babies and have been around them my whole life. This was not the first newborn I ever held. I knew that generally their little bodies stay together as they are lifted.

I mentioned her floppiness to the nurse and doctor and how weak her sucking was. They dismissed my concerns and told me she was perfect, that she was just loose-jointed. So I tried to believe them. They were the trained professionals, so they knew far more than me, right? I asked why she was too weak to nurse and why it took ninety minutes to drink three ounces from a bottle. I was told she was fine, gaining and growing well. I was just a first-time mom prone to worry.

Andrea also slept through the night from the day I brought her home from the hospital. I thought that was odd, but the doctors just told me to wake her every three or four hours to feed. The sleeping was probably just a bonus, but taken together with my other concerns, was there more? Doctors seemed to address each individual concern, but I did not feel that they were seeing the whole picture.

Andrea smiled right on schedule, but every other developmental milestone was delayed. At each doctor visit, I would ask, "Why isn't she rolling over, reaching, grabbing, crawling, standing, or walking?" I had read every child development book I could find and took human development and early childhood education classes in college. I knew—I felt—something was amiss.

But with every appointment and every question, I received the same answers: "She is fine. A little delayed but within normal limits. This is your first baby, and new moms tend to overreact with their first."

Even friends and family were telling me I was being over the top and that everything seemed normal and fine to them. Relatives told me to quit reading so many books and that the information in them was causing me to expect Andrea to adhere to the developmental charts. No. I didn't care if she were developing on some science-based timeline. I didn't care if she were late or early in doing anything. But my gut said something was not right, and I could not make that feeling go away.

Parents, please trust your instincts. We are told that so many times, but oftentimes health-care professionals can be dismissive of a mom's instincts. Family members love your child but sometimes only see what they want to see. Cliché as it sounds, it is true: nobody knows your child like you do.

Andrea's milestones were reached at the absolute end of what the charts call "normal limits." So because according to the charts she fell within the normal range, she was considered normal, and my concerns were not addressed. I was told each child develops according to a predetermined schedule that is unique to each of them. I agreed. But still I knew.

I had other concerns. She did not cue me, as babies do, as to when she was full. She would continue to eat and drink until she projectile vomited. The doctors simply said I would need to determine when she had eaten enough and stop feeding her since she never turned away from the bottle or pushed the spoon away. She had tongue thrusting, and it took several attempts to get a full spoonful of baby food into her. The doctors told me what an average amount of food and milk for a baby at each stage was, and that was how I knew when to stop her feedings.

"But is that normal to not know when to stop?" I would ask.

"It's of no real concern," they'd answer. "She is gaining and developing normally."

Andrea also had tactile defensiveness since birth. She was not comforted by swaddling, rocking, or body contact. In fact, she seemed agitated and uncomfortable with it. So I would lay her on a blanket and prop books, stuffed animals, and musical toys around her. Then I'd lay on the floor with her and talk to her. That brought her the most comfort.

Again, I'd ask, "Is that normal?"

"Every baby is different. Not all babies like to be swaddled," I was told.

I persisted, "But it's not just swaddling. She is sensitive to any touch and does not like it. She seems bothered by movement like rocking or swinging."

The doctor did not seem concerned by any of this. I questioned myself after every appointment, *Maybe they're right. I might be overreacting to every little thing. I need to just relax and enjoy this baby.*

Andrea's gross and fine motor skills were seriously delayed as her whole body was very weak and her muscle tone was poor. At one point, a doctor suggested she could have ataxic cerebral palsy. I asked for further testing, but no further investigation was done. I was told that no test confirms or rules out ataxic cerebral palsy and it is extremely difficult to diagnose. This made no sense. If there were no way to really know, then why are some diagnosed with it and others are not?

I took her from doctor to doctor and was given the same answers. I asked for a complete assessment. I wanted her evaluated by specialists and wanted my concerns to be addressed in more depth. My insurance was such that each referral had to be done by the primary doctor. I was told that an assessment like I was asking for would mean multiple referrals, and the doctor did not feel any of them were necessary. At this point in time, I did not know about Regional Center.

At around eighteen months, I noticed she was not hearing well, not responding to sounds appropriately. She had no interest in TV or musical toys, but she did have a passive vocabulary as her favorite thing to do was to sit next to me on the couch and read picture books. I would name an object; she would point to it. It was her all-time favorite activity, and she did not lose interest as we went through book after book doing this. I was confused. I thought she had a hearing problem, yet she understood my speech.

Finally at age two, I brought her to yet another pediatrician and said, "Look, my daughter is two years old. She cannot speak. She can't run or jump. She can't feed herself and drools profusely. Please help us! Something is wrong, and the clock is ticking!"

I can still see her in my mind's eye at that appointment. She was sitting in a chair in the doctor's office wearing a little pink summer dress, mouth open, big eyes staring at me. It was like she was saying, "I'm sorry. I am doing my best. Is something wrong with me?"

From that moment on, even though Andrea wasn't yet speaking, I knew she had a large passive vocabulary and an understanding for much of what was being said in her presence, and I determined to never again discuss anything negative about her development in front of her.

Doctors and therapists were not as sensitive to this, and over the years, I often had to ask or remind them to please not say that in front of Andrea.

The new pediatrician only looked at her, did a quick exam, and said, "I agree. We have a problem here."

Time changed to warp speed and continued that way for many years. The doctor referred us to Regional Center for the developmentally disabled and advised that I follow their instructions. He also wanted Andrea seen by an ENT for hearing, along with an evaluation by a speech pathologist, physical therapist, occupational therapist, and neurologist. I left his office with a stack of referrals and appointments to make.

I left his office with a heavy heart. Although I had been hoping a doctor would confirm that I wasn't crazy, when it did finally happen, I had my moment of sorrow, to be sure. Part of me always hoped the doctors were right and I was wrong. The other part of me was relieved that the ball was now rolling and Andrea could begin to get the help she needed.

I am not sure when you got the news about your child. Was it in utero? At birth? Months later? Years later? Usually it is a piece-by-piece revelation that reveals your child's physical and mental challenges, little by little. God is so gracious. If we knew everything all at once, we may not be able to handle it, so instead He gives us the information in bite-sized pieces.

Even so, this news is followed by a grieving of sorts. We

grieve over the loss of our vision and expectations. We all hope for a happy, healthy child who can grow and develop normally. We see that before he is ever born and anticipate the joy of it all. So when the news is delivered that it will not be as we imagined, we grieve over the lost dream and the potential struggles our child must now face.

This day began years of endless appointments, therapies, surgeries, meetings, IEPs, and sometimes demanding that she receive what she needed and was entitled to have. For us parents, this is a full-on period of education. Andrea never received a formal diagnosis such as autism, cerebral palsy, down syndrome, or Asperger's syndrome. It would have been much easier if she had. I was only told she had characteristics of autism and cerebral palsy, but not enough of any one to result in a diagnosis. So many children and adults with disabilities fall through the cracks of the system, as Andrea has.

What is the first question you are asked when seeking help for your child? It is always, "What is the diagnosis?" When you are unable to answer that but simply must describe the child, you are told repeatedly that unless they are diagnosed with a specific disorder or syndrome, you do not qualify. There was nothing in writing from any doctor or test that provided what most agencies were asking for. If your child falls into this category, I sympathize, as you will likely need to fight, plead, and pray for every door that needs to be opened for them.

Don't ever give up. Keep a journal and take detailed

notes, dates, doctors, and decisions. Note the age that your child reaches each milestone. You will most likely need this information in the future. I suggest that you take your child to every appointment you are trying to get services with, as often how a child looks on paper is nothing like how they appear in real time.

Andrea was accepted by Regional Center for the developmentally disabled at age two, but by age five, she tested average on IQ tests, so she no longer qualified for their program. She no longer qualified for any program, so special education was all we had. She was placed in the communicatively handicapped program with the city schools. I was pleased that they provided the services she needed, and her doctors referred her to Children's Hospital for additional therapies, including speech, OT, and PT. But doctors and insurance will only approve a set number of visits. It is usually not ongoing, although that is exactly what was needed. So now what?

Over the years, Andrea had many IQ tests, and looking at the scores now, they ranged from 85 to 98. What does all that mean? The population in the United States has an average IQ of 98. Other countries have average scores of anywhere from 84 to 100. Who cares? Should we care? Much of the test is about spatial integration, in puzzle form, so Andrea would score extremely low in this area, and other parts involved visual memory, again extremely low. The auditory memory portion was sky-high though (when she was wearing her hearing aids).

So the psychologist would take those numbers, average them out, and call it her IQ. This disqualified her from many programs. But an IQ score does not describe or define a person, and it rarely helps us understand them.

Regional Center requires that an individual have an intellectual disability, epilepsy, cerebral palsy, or autism. She no longer qualified. The Arc is for those with intellectual and developmental disabilities. She did not qualify. California Children's Services covers many services and may be able to help your child with medical expenses. Andrea did not qualify.

United Cerebral Palsy is a wonderful program with many support services. She did not qualify. Easter Seals offers resources for autism and many other disabilities. You may apply for grants to get help with programs or equipment your child may need. We did not pursue this.

One of Andrea's therapists recommended the Shriners to help pay for her hearing aids. We did not pursue this either, as we were blessed to be able to afford them ourselves. There are many other wonderful programs and parent support groups that can be investigated if you feel the need to do so. Parent to Parent USA, National Youth Leadership Network, National Collaborative on Workforce and Disability for Youth, The M.O.R.G.A.N. Project, Federation for Children with Special Needs, National Dissemination Center for Children with Disabilities, Family Voices, National Parent Technical Assistance Center, Council for Exceptional Children, and Disabled Sports USA are a few. If your child is in special education through your school system, the IEP team is a great resource to help direct you to the outside sources that may benefit your child the most.

It is key to remember three federal laws that protect the rights of people with disabilities: the Americans with Disabilities Act (ADA), the Individuals with Disabilities Education Act (IDEA), and Section 504 of the Rehabilitation Act. Congress enacted the Education for All Handicapped Children Act (Public Law 94-142) in 1975 to support states and localities in protecting the rights of, meeting the individual needs of, and improving the results for infants, toddlers, children, and youth with disabilities and their families. IDEA represents the pinnacle of the equal education movement. This law has roots in the same civil rights movement that gave rise to *Brown vs. Board of Education*. It is legislation that ensures students with a disability are given free appropriate public education tailored to their individual needs.

This information became vital for me later as Andrea began to be denied the services she needed. Because Andrea had no actual diagnosis and therefore was not accepted by any special needs agencies other than the Department of Rehabilitation, I had to do some homework. I spent hours and hours at an area university in their medical library researching all of her borderline diagnoses. I am so grateful that this library allows public access although no books could be taken from the premises.

Remember, this was before home computers, access to Google, and smartphones. We had libraries.

I read and took notes on everything relative to Andrea's needs. I learned she had sensory integration disorders. She struggled with spatial judgment and awareness. She had gross and fine motor delays, problems with balance and knowing left from right, visual memory problems, sensitivity to movement of all kinds, tactile defensiveness, and a multitude of other issues, including hearing and language problems and difficulty with visual tracking and judging distance. Her therapists, teachers, and IEP teams confirmed these many disorders and challenges over the years. Unfortunately none of these qualified her for the programs or services she so desperately needed. These were her challenges, but they were not a diagnosis.

I was convinced after much reading and study that Andrea had a mild form of ataxic cerebral palsy and possibly a mild form of autism, although we never received a formal diagnosis of this from a doctor. But as I researched, I learned that cerebral palsy is a neurological disorder that affects body movement and muscle coordination. It usually appears in infancy or early childhood. It may take a baby with cerebral palsy longer than usual to start rolling over, sitting up, crawling, or walking. It can be mild or severe. There may be excessive drooling, hearing loss, trouble learning to speak, and difficulties with fine motor skills. Ataxic cerebral palsy displays itself in low muscle tone. It affects balance, coordination, and depth perception. Some of the risk factors are exposure to toxic substances by the pregnant mother and babies in a feet-first (breech) position at the beginning of labor. Check every box. Every one of these indicators applied to Andrea.

Having a child with challenges can sometimes feel like a science project or notebook of chores and goals to reach. I remember wishing I could just sit on the floor with her and have carefree play, but instead I would sit on the floor with her and work on the next goal, the next milestone or skill we were trying to achieve. I realized I was missing the moment. I did not learn this overnight. I had to deliberately change my approach and make a choice to have fun! I learned to celebrate the tiniest bits of progress and know that each step was a building block for the next and worth celebrating. Rather than keeping my eye on the result, I learned to find joy in the process.

As parents, our different children help us grow in knowledge, but more importantly, they help us to grow in character and grace. I am not by nature an assertive person. But Andrea has taught me to advocate fiercely for her. I have never wanted to schedule more than one or two appointments per day, but Andrea has taught me to schedule jam-packed days with back-to-back appointments and never miss a beat. I also never took the initiative to greet a disabled person in the same way I would a nondisabled person.

But Andrea taught me that the one common denominator in all people are feelings. All people want to be acknowledged and accepted. Nobody likes to feel ignored or invisible. It is no longer out of my comfort zone to make eye contact with anyone and ask how they are doing and engage them in conversation. That is a far cry from a little smile, nod, or look-the-other-way response. She has taught me patience, perseverance, and compassion. Little wonder our children are called "gifts."

Water

> "For I will pour water on the thirsty land, and streams on the dry ground; I will pour out my Spirit on your offspring, and my blessing on your descendants."
>
> —Isaiah 44:3 (NIV)

I was gifted with three more daughters after Andrea: Joy in 1982, Sarah in 1988, and Carly in 1992. I was amazed how easy it was to raise a child without Andrea's challenges. They simply moved from stage to stage all on their own. It was a joy to watch them all develop so naturally and with so little intervention. Each was so incredibly different from the other. Sometimes I felt like I was morphing into four different people moment by moment to match where they each were developmentally. It was a challenging and wonderful time. Subsequent children have a somewhat different environment than the first. I read a quote by Nicole Fornabaio that is quite accurate. "'Can he have this?'

With the first baby: 'Is it organic and homemade?' After second baby: 'He can have anything except narcotics and alcohol.'"

I also realized after having the other three girls how little attention Andrea received from the world. Perhaps you have experienced the same. Strangers would ooh and ahh and coo at my daughters, talk to them, smile at them, and fully engage with them. In contrast, when Andrea was a baby, strangers did not do this. Generally they looked the other way. She did have a different look. She drooled until third grade because of her weak facial muscles and made loud repetitive sounds as a baby.

I don't fault these people for not approaching Andrea in the same way. Andrea's differences made them uncomfortable. I get it. Sometimes though, what we don't do has a bigger impact than what we do. This hurt me emotionally, and it hurt Andrea socially. While other babies are lavished by attention from the world, and by it, they learn to be socially interactive and appropriate. Our different children are often largely ignored and miss these opportunities to develop normally in the social arena. It really does take a village.

Pre-Andrea, I was guilty of the same behaviors. Post-Andrea, I go out of my way to approach the different, the forgotten, or the ignored. It is more important that we do this for them than for others, as few people do, and it is an undeniable need of our human hearts to be accepted and recognized, yes, even for babies.

I remember one elderly woman in a grocery store line asking me, "What's wrong with her?" as Andrea sat in the shopping cart making her loud sounds, drooling, and staring at nothing. I did not know what to say. Remember, she was never given a diagnosis or label, so what do you tell people?

I just answered, "What do you mean?"

She said, "Well, her mouth is hanging open. You should teach her to close it."

I politely answered that she had weak muscles in her face and couldn't do that yet. The woman just looked away, and my heart broke again.

"Forget what hurt you in the past, but never forget what it taught you" (Shannon L. Adler).

I understand the pain and rejection you feel each time your child is treated in this way. It is far worse than if it had happened to you. But in retrospect, God wastes no opportunity to grow us, and in these many instances when we experience this pain through our children, God is softening and enlarging our hearts for others. Because of these rejections, we learn to open our arms wide to the lonely, rejected, overlooked, or different people of the world. And through this growth in ourselves, our children are given an even better role model to do the same. Ultimately I thank God for the people who have crossed our path and stretched us to become better parents and better human beings. And so it begins. We start to change this world one person and one interaction at a time.

While waiting for an opening in the public school program, Regional Center strongly advised that I get Andrea enrolled in a private preschool as soon as possible. I enrolled her in a local preschool with remarkably high ratings and recommendations. Andrea separated reasonably well the first day and joined the group easily, but as the weeks went on, she became increasingly distressed when I would tell her she got to go to school today. I sat in to observe the class several times and could not understand why she did not want to go, as during my observation it all seemed pleasant enough.

I decided to arrive earlier than usual one day. To my horror, the children were all in the outside play area, and four of them were throwing toys at and piling their little bodies up on my Andrea. I continued to watch as the teacher called the children to another activity, leaving Andrea alone on the far side of the play area whimpering and trying to self-comfort. Still I watched to see if she would recover on her own and join the group or be encouraged to. It went against every instinct I had to not rush in and rescue her.

But God was training me early on to stand down until intervention was necessary. A few more minutes was all I needed. The teacher engaged all the other children in a new activity without a single gesture of comfort to Andrea, nor an invitation for her to participate or any instruction to the children that what they had done to Andrea was wrong. That was all I needed to see. I got my daughter, left, and never returned. I demanded a full refund of the tuition and got it.

Yes, bullying begins at the toddler level. Children seem to have an intuitive sense about who the weak link is. For a child with already impaired social skills, bullying can have a lifelong impact. A survey done in 2015 showed that 50 percent of special needs children experienced bullying during their school day. Of those 50 percent, a staggering 94 percent reported that there had been multiple incidents of bullying. This is a dire situation, as all studies have found that children with disabilities were two to three times more likely to be victims of bullying than their non-disabled peers.

We parents walk a fine line in trying to determine when to rescue our children and when to back off and allow them to learn to handle these situations on their own. In the case of bullying—and this did occur often through the years—I found it best to talk to the school, the teacher, and the playground monitor, but mostly to Andrea.

In the beginning, Andrea would just cower, let it happen, and then try to recover from it on her own. I worked with her and role-played situations as she got older, teaching her to look me in the eye and firmly say, "Stop it!" If that did not work, which it usually didn't, I taught her to find the nearest adult to assist. And I made her promise to tell me always, always!

I explained to Andrea that we needed to help that person (bully) to learn that their behavior was wrong and unkind, and if nobody noticed or pointed that out, they would grow into an even bigger and more menacing bully. With direction, Andrea is able to put others before herself, so using this psychology with her seemed to motivate her to report incidents more easily.

Andrea came home from school in third grade and said, "Someone called me a disabled. What's a disabled?" I had always avoided using the word *disabled* about Andrea. I just never felt there was any benefit in referring to her this way. And honestly I never saw her this way. But now there was the question.

"Lord, give me wisdom. Help me give her the right answer." I explained that everyone was able and everyone was disabled. She was no exception. I gave examples within the family, especially as they applied to the word *disabled*. I told her that I was disabled when it came to public speaking, meaning this was a challenge, difficult, nearly impossible for me. Her sister was disabled in speaking directly to people, meaning she was extremely shy and always looked down when speaking to people. Andrea beamed. She absolutely loved knowing that she was not alone in this category.

She asked how she was disabled. I told her that she was challenged with clear speech and doing PE activities. I explained that just because something was hard, it did not mean we could not overcome it and then no longer be disabled in this area, but for everyone, some things were easy and other things were hard. The question never came up again, and Andrea seemed smugly satisfied with my answer.

There were several times while growing Andrea that the mama bear in me rose in rage. In fact, I don't think I ever experienced the emotion of rage until it involved my children being hurt. I have no doubt that you have experienced the same.

I was picking up Andrea from middle school one day when I noticed two boys in her age group walking behind her, laughing, and imitating her unusual gait. Andrea began to walk faster, and the faster she walked, the more pronounced her odd walk became. She sometimes looked like she was swimming with her arms as she went down the street, and at best, she would swing her arms wildly. It was obviously different.

I parked across the street and honked for her to come get in the car, but she either didn't hear or was so focused on what was happening that she didn't notice. The boys got closer, louder, and more mocking. I made a U-turn and pulled up beside Andrea for her to hop in the car. I glared at the boys as they passed us, and then I followed them home! Oh, yes, I did! So much for that fine line we walk.

I watched them both enter a house about two blocks later, parked my car, and got out. Andrea was begging me, "Don't talk to them, Mom! No, don't!"

I told her I would only be a minute and she needed to wait in the car. I walked up to the house and knocked. No answer. I knocked again. No answer. I then pounded on the door repeatedly until one of the boys answered. I asked if his parents were home, to which he answered, "No, they are at work."

I asked for the boy to get his friend, brother, or whoever that other boy was because I would like to talk to them both. Soon I had them both standing before me looking terrified. I told them that school rules apply right up until the moment they are safely home from school, so what they did today was against school rules. I told them I would be watching them, and if another incident like this occurred, I would report them to their principal and their parents. And then I looked closer, and something in me softened. I explained that we are each made differently.

I asked them, "If you had been born the same as Andrea, how would you want to be treated?" I explained that she could not help the way she walks and she was blessed to be able to walk at all. The boys engaged in a short conversation with me, and I explained what was hard for Andrea and why. They asked valid questions about her. I could tell they were not bad kids. They were junior-high boys who likely got caught up in each other's wrong choices. In the end, they apologized. I asked them to step one rung higher, and if they ever saw Andrea or anyone else being made fun of, they would step in and stop it. They promised to do that. We can change the world!

Another incident occurred when Andrea was fourteen years old. I had her and her three sisters with me at a photo studio in our community, waiting to have their pictures taken. A group of teens was waiting also, and they were snickering, laughing, and gesturing toward Andrea. Here we go again. That rage rose in me.

I told the girls to wait right there, and I took the baby with me. I approached the group of about five and asked them to step outside with me for a moment, which they did. I don't know. Was that even legal?

But they obliged and followed me outside. I admit I had anger in my voice as I told them, "Be careful about how you label other people. I heard you. Andrea is hearing impaired and has weak muscles. Her feelings are no different than yours (although Andrea did not hear the remarks made). Remember that!" I told them they could go back in now, and they all sat down quietly. I will never know if that confrontation had any impact on those children. I do know I could not sit passively and say nothing.

I often thought about how Andrea's world must look when I am not around. If these incidents occurred so often in my presence, what did her day-to-day life look like? I knew it couldn't be easy. I prayed harder than ever for her protection and ability to deflect these assaults.

"The prettiest smiles hide the deepest secrets, the prettiest eyes have cried the most tears, and the kindest hearts have felt the most pain" (Author Unknown).

Growth

> "Let your roots grow down into him, and let
> your lives be built on him. Then your faith
> will grow strong in the truth you were taught,
> and you will overflow with thankfulness."
>
> —Colossians 2:7 (NLT)

Special education began for Andrea when she was two and a half years old. Regional Center suggested the most optimal path to stimulate her development would be an infant-development program with the city schools in our hometown. So the little yellow bus would stop in front of our house to get Andrea, her car seat, her diaper bag, and supplies. I recall the first day she took that bus thinking, *What have I done? I've never left her with a babysitter, yet I'm entrusting her to a stranger?*

It took every ounce of willpower to walk back into the house and not jump in my car to follow that bus. Andrea took it all in stride though and just waved goodbye. Meanwhile, I paced the floor and stared at the clock until her safe return.

It proved to be a wonderful program with a loving and caring teacher. Andrea was exposed to a plethora of sensory stimulation and activities, fine and gross motor goals, and tasks, along with a happy environment. The staff quickly learned that she took no comfort in hugs and touch, so they would smile and give her verbal affirmation instead.

Andrea responded well, and by the age of five, she no longer qualified for Regional Center, and I allowed them to remove her as a client. In retrospect, I should not have done that, but I made my share of mistakes, to be sure. To me, it often seemed like a trial-and-error process raising children.

When Andrea was four years old, she tested with a severe hearing loss in both ears. She was fitted with hearing aids, and I will never forget the first time we turned on the television to *Sesame Street* wearing those aids. She reeled around, looked at the TV, sat down on the floor, and was mesmerized by it all. She noticed everything and was able to finally hear sounds she had never heard before. It was so exciting to see her becoming so alert and attentive to her new world of clear sound. Her hearing loss is progressive, and each year, she is losing more and more of her hearing. She may possibly be in a silent world someday. But today she is not, and today is where we live.

I was told by several therapists when Andrea was four years old that she would always be clumsy and messy and her muscles would always be less than average in strength and tone. And because her brain was disorganized, that would translate to her external world also being messy and disorganized. I remember thinking, *Not my kid.*

I care very much about neatness and order, so I was certain I could teach her to be somewhat organized. Andrea is now forty-one years old, and although I would love to tell you I succeeded in this, I admit I have not. Even labeling bins, simplifying her room, and creating minimal clutter is a constant mess. I can completely clean and organize her room, and within twenty-four hours, it is in disarray. I have asked her if she likes it that way, and she tells me, "No, I like it neat." And yet she is completely unaware as it begins to get out of control.

She will write in a journal, toss it and her pen to the floor, grab another journal, do the same, get gel pens, work on a project, and forget where she laid the caps or even where she put the project. And so it goes. I always preach, "Never give up."

I confess I have given up in this area. I now work with her a few times a year to put her room back in shape, reminding her to keep it that way, only to watch it disintegrate quickly. The rest of the time, the rule is "keep your bedroom door closed."

Even though she is clueless about some things like organization, she is rigid and literal in the world of rules. If it says stop, you stop. If it says go, you go. There are no exceptions, no gray areas. All rules are black and white. This made it amazingly easy to train and discipline her, but there were times I didn't care for it at all.

I remember the time I was making a turn at a sign that clearly said, "No Left Turn." I read the sign out loud and said out loud, "There's not a soul on this street in any direction. I'm turning left. Otherwise I have to go two more blocks to make a U-turn."

So left I went, and out of nowhere came a police car, siren screeching and lights flashing. *Ohhhh, no way*, I thought. I had never had a ticket in my life.

I pulled over, and the officer approached my car and asked first and foremost, "Did you see the sign that said 'no left turn'?"

I thought, *He's giving me an out! I just have to say I never saw it.* In all honesty, I desperately wanted to say, "Really? No, sir, I didn't see that!" But I would never get away with it. I had Andrea with me, the ultimate cop, and she would have blurted out the truth as loudly as possible.

So I simply said, "Yes, I saw it," and he proceeded to issue me a ticket. Thanks, Andrea.

As I pulled back out after this little joy ride, I told Andrea, "I can't believe I got a ticket!"

She looked at me incredulously, "Well, you broke the law, Mom!"

Umm, yeah, I did. I also scored zero as a role model that day.

By kindergarten, Andrea was placed in the Communicatively Handicapped Program and bussed to a school about ten miles from our home that started at 8:00 a.m. and ended at 2:30 p.m. Most school days though, she had either speech or physical therapy before school at Children's Hospital, and I would drive her from therapy to school and then wait for her bus in the afternoon, as this exhausted child would arrive home to an enormous amount of homework. We usually worked together on that after a snack for at least an hour a day and then dinner, more homework, bath, and bed. Her school days could be more grueling than the average adult's workday.

I became concerned that there was no time for play. There was no time to go outside with the other children and develop some social skills. Her teacher told me that could come later. At this stage of development, learning to speak clearly and catch up academically was far more important. But I knew she was at a critical stage for learning social skills and interacting freely with other children. I felt she was missing so much, and she was always exhausted.

As her kindergarten year went on, she began to resist going to school, get sick more often, and cry more and more. I volunteered in her classroom and was upset again by what I saw. Andrea struggled to hold a pencil, as she had extremely poor fine motor skills. She would often drop it, and eventually we taped it to her hand so she could attempt to learn writing. I witnessed the teacher checking her work, slamming her hand on the paper, tearing it up, giving her a new page, and saying, "Do it again. This is bad! You're bad!"

My heart was ripped from me. I wanted to cry right then and there, but I saw that Andrea didn't. She just tried again. "Oh, Lord, give me the right words and attitude." I prayed. I confronted the teacher at the end of the school day. I told her that Andrea had made great strides in her class, but I also wanted her to please understand how terribly long her day was and how easily she tired. I told her teacher that I understood she had her methods, but I wanted to make it clear that she was never to call my child "bad."

I said, "I do not believe Andrea gives anything but her best, so to ask her to do it again is one thing. To raise the bar is fine, but never, ever call her out like that again."

The teacher agreed, and even though the year started with conflict between the teacher and me, it ended with a beautiful, cooperative friendship and mutual goal to give Andrea the best education possible. Ultimately I loved this teacher and requested her for first grade also. Andrea also bonded with her.

We were even invited to her wedding the following year, a wedding in which no children were invited, mind you. What an honor. I tell you this story to help you to be mindful that each of your child's teachers will be different and have a different approach. Some will be better than others. But if you work with them and not against them, this will always benefit your child.

Teaching is no easy career path. Always assume the teacher wants your child to succeed. It is so important to know what happens in the classroom. Observe not only the teacher, but your child's responses and behaviors. It is an entirely different environment than home, and there is so much you can learn to further help your child.

I was not pleased with the progress Andrea was making

in her speech. She was still 90 percent unintelligible by age five, so we hired a private speech therapist to come to the home twice a week. I will never forget her. She not only worked on making specific speech sounds, but she also quickly noted that Andrea's oral and facial muscles would not allow her to do this. So in the beginning, she focused on stimulating her tongue, cheeks, and palate. She worked on strengthening the muscles she needed for speech. As I have stated, Andrea had tactile and sensory problems, so she literally could not tell what her mouth was doing. Nor could she feel what she needed to feel in order to make a "t" sound, for example.

The therapist set up a mirror so Andrea could see just where her tongue needed to be placed to reproduce a specific sound. Not only did the therapist use the right approach with her, but she was also highly animated and made it fun for Andrea. She also taught me what to do on the days she was not there.

So Andrea, the therapist, and I worked the entire summer between kindergarten and first grade, and she made huge strides. By the time she started first grade, she tested as only 10 percent unintelligible, and her teacher was astounded! This brought Andrea miles ahead in self-esteem and social interactions too, as you can well imagine.

Up until this point, Andrea would use lots of gesturing and gibberish to communicate what she wanted or needed. I have no idea how, but I understood her, and we would have complete conversations like this while others looked on like we were both aliens, speaking another-world language. If someone asked Andrea a question, she would look at me as she answered it so I could translate for her. This was how we rolled. This was not going to work long term. So all of us rejoiced in her ability to learn to speak more clearly.

Andrea continued to make good strides academically, and by the end of first grade, she was reading and doing math above her grade level. My concern at this age was that she talked to herself aloud in the classroom. This was always an independent education plan (IEP) goal to cue her to stop doing that, but it was never achieved.

I was also troubled that Andrea still had great difficulty with balance, coordination, and fine motor skills. I had read a wonderful book called *Sensory Integration and the Child* by Anna Jean Ayres and learned that much of this has to do with the semicircular canals of the inner ear, and if stimulated and moved correctly, this would translate to improvement in all the areas of my concern. This was part of occupational therapy, so at the IEP the year Andrea was nine, I requested more OT. It was denied.

I refused to sign the IEP, as I was not in agreement with the education plan if it did not include this therapy. I had learned, as is true with all areas of development, that there is a critical period to achieve results, and with sensory issues, it is up until the age of ten that optimal progress can be made. After that, it takes twice as long to achieve half as much.

Being aware of the Individuals with Disabilities Education Act (IDEA), a federal law requiring schools to serve the educational needs of eligible students with disabilities, I knew Andrea had a right to this therapy. I secured a parent facilitator from our city schools, and together we applied to Sacramento for a hearing. A team from the State of California Board of Education came to our school district, where we lived, and we discussed the dispute. It was a little scary, no doubt about that, but I had the reports in hand from therapists and teachers, stating how much Andrea could benefit from having this therapy. It was mandated that Andrea receive this therapy for the next school year and be reevaluated again at the time of the next IEP. I was ecstatic. This was such an important year, and we had won.

Parents, if you do not agree with the education plan for your child, you have every right to disagree and refuse to sign the IEP, which, by signing, you agree to. You can dispute this with a hearing involving the Board of Education, and if that does not achieve the results your child needs, you can appeal that decision all the way to the state or federal courts. Nobody likes to push against the grain, or fight for something, less than I do. This is the last thing I ever want to do, but always keeping your child's best interests in mind, you may sometimes have to. There is help and guidance for you.

We had recently bought a new and larger home, and my husband was happy to have a two-car garage where he could place his tools and do projects and woodworking. This coincided with Andrea's occupational therapy and the suggestion that we create a gym of sorts for her at home so her therapy could extend from one day a week to seven days a week.

I must give credit where it is due. He gave up his dream of having a workshop in lieu of creating the optimal environment for Andrea to do her therapies. He hung a hammock, a barrel, a large workout ball, and other apparatus for her to exercise on. The goal of this therapy is to create movement in every direction that the semicircular canals of the inner ear flow. So she would lie prone and be pushed, as in a swing. She would be spun around and lie on her back and side, every direction possible, helping to stimulate those canals and develop better balance and coordination.

It is interesting to observe that normal children naturally do these movements during play. They do all sorts of crazy and daring movements on swings and jungle gyms and just intuitively know what sorts of movement they need to develop correctly. On the contrary, Andrea desperately needed these movements but avoided them at all costs.

The therapy and supplemental garage therapy helped tremendously. At this juncture in time, a twelve-year-old neighbor girl named Lacie would stop by daily after school and help me with Andrea's therapy. She was a godsend. Lacie helped to make Andrea feel as though she were playing with friends rather than working, and as a result, she worked extremely hard on the equipment and exercises. The outcome was good. She had better balance and coordination and improved strength in her core.

By the end of fifth grade, I decided with the full agreement of the IEP team to mainstream her. Rather than start her in sixth grade, I had her repeat fifth grade in a regular class. Prior to Andrea's first day, the regular classroom teacher first prepared the class by explaining what Andrea's differences were and how they all might make this transition easier for her. The teacher even played a recording of what a classroom and teacher sounds like to a person with Andrea's hearing loss. The recording showed the class how a student like Andrea would catch some, but not all, of what is said. It was, therefore, understandable if the student's responses and answers were wrong or inappropriate at times.

The teacher did an excellent job, and Andrea's transition into regular school was seamless and uneventful. Andrea was happy to be going to school right down the street and bragged to friends and family that she was in regular school now. She continued to have adaptive PE and resource help, and extra time was allowed for her to take tests. These additional compensations followed her throughout the rest of her school years right up to graduation.

Ninth grade was a challenging one. Andrea became depressed and withdrawn. It was so worrisome for me to see my typically happy, animated daughter become so quiet and sad. God is good at every juncture and has always stepped in for Andrea at the exact right moment. A friend of mine, who was also a special education teacher, suggested Andrea do some peer tutoring for her in her severely handicapped class. She even received a credit toward graduation for it.

So from tenth through twelfth grades, one period per day, Andrea would go to her class and help the other students with whatever tasks they were assigned, whether it was learning to read, count, or some other basic skill. This teacher later recounted that Andrea was very well-liked by the students and that Andrea had a natural ability to break down a task to its simplest form for the students to succeed. In the process of helping these kids, Andrea came alive. She was happy again, her confidence soared, and she looked forward to school, particularly this class. She felt needed and liked.

When Andrea was a senior, she was required to pass a test in government, without which a diploma would not be awarded. She studied constantly. She memorized the Bill of Rights, various laws, government branches, and terminology. We made flash cards with a word on the front and a definition on the back. For an entire semester, she carried these everywhere, even drilling herself during car rides. All students were allowed up to three attempts to pass the test in government. Andrea passed on the first try. She also qualified for the workability program, which provides vocational training to high school students. She worked at an after-school daycare program several days a week and loved it. She was helping students with homework and supervising their outdoor play. She had hoped to be hired for this work after graduation, but sadly they had to let her go, as she could not fulfill all the job requirements, one of which required physical strength in helping the kids on the playground.

Andrea graduated with a high school diploma, not a certificate. She earned a low B average in all regular classes. I did not cry at her graduation ceremony. I sobbed. What a glorious day that was. We had a party to beat all parties, and Andrea beamed with pride.

Since Andrea had so loved helping in the severely handicapped class during high school, I thought this was a perfect fit for her to pursue as an occupation. A special education technician is a paid position with the city school system, so I took Andrea downtown to the Board of Education to apply. She first had to pass a test that measured her reading, writing, and math abilities. She passed all but the math, which she missed by two points. She repeated the test in six months with the same score.

I told her, "That's ok. We'll try again, but first let's polish up your math."

So she started community college and earned Bs and Cs for the next two years, but unfortunately she could not go further, as the classes she needed required prerequisites that were simply too difficult for her to pass. She stopped going to college and went back to test with the city schools. Her scores did not change, so she could not apply. Two tiny points. Even though she took math in college to refresh her and enable her to pass the test, that two-point discrepancy remained. She began looking for a job and sending out résumés.

At this point, we worked with the California State Department of Rehabilitation, but sadly they were unable to find appropriate work for Andrea. Rather they taught résumé skills and helped her do mock interviews, and then she was on her own, competing with the rest of the world for a job. She submitted her résumé to childcare facilities, preschools, stores, and anywhere she could potentially work. She rarely got an interview, and when she did, she was told they had chosen another candidate. I told her not to get discouraged, but clearly she was.

This period coincided with my second daughter's graduation, my third daughter beginning to abuse alcohol and drugs, my fourth daughter still in elementary school, divorce, and the loss of my mother to pancreatic cancer. Andrea was discouraged, I was overwhelmed, and both of us were sad. In many ways, Andrea was put on hold for several years while other priorities took my time, attention, and energy.

Darkness

> "I create the light and make the darkness. I
> send good times and bad times. I, the LORD,
> am the one who does these things."
>
> —Isaiah 45:7 (NLT)

Growth cannot continue in the dark, and there was a dark period where progress was dormant for Andrea. In a three-year period, we experienced the loss of our dear pastor, my marriage, and my mother, who was a vital part of our lives, in that order. I was so despondent at one point I thought how much easier it would be when we are all done with this world. At that moment, I clearly heard God say, "Be still, and know that I am God" (Psalm 46:10 NIV). Complete peace came over me, and I took each day one at a time and coped the best I could.

Alcoholism is a dreadful and progressive disease that destroys the individual addict and affects the entire family. Andrea's father was a good, intelligent, successful man who had provided well for his family all these many years, but the demon of addiction was destroying and changing him into someone we did not know. And it was changing our family.

So I took the girls and myself to Al-Anon and learned I had made many mistakes in handling this. I learned I had no control. I learned that asking an alcoholic to stop drinking is like asking a pneumonia patient to stop coughing. Neither can do it without treatment. So I begged him to go to AA, which he did for about a month but then decided it was not for him.

We went to several marriage counselors who all stated that this marriage was doomed if the drinking did not stop. Still I did not give up. I did not believe in divorce. I did not want my children to go through the long-term aftermath of divorce. The girls were all showing effects of the darkness that had come into our home, so I took them all to counseling.

I remember the day the counselor asked to meet with all five of us rather than individually and asked, "How many of you think it might be a good idea if your mom asked your dad to leave the home for a while?"

I watched in shock as all four of them raised their hand at once. We did not fight and argue in front of them, so they had not had to experience that. I learned a long time ago to not engage with a person who is drunk or angry. Fighting and arguing cannot exist in a vacuum. But the unpredictability of an alcoholic parent takes its toll. They never knew if Daddy would come home, happy, mad, sad, or quiet. They never knew when or if Daddy would come home on time or at all, and the predictable family mealtimes that had once been so important to us all were few and far between now.

Still I did not want to give up. I sought counseling from my pastor and other believers, who all said, "It's ok to leave." There were actions and behaviors that allowed divorce, biblically. Still I had not heard it from God Himself.

One evening, I went into the bathroom with my Bible, locked the door, and begged God to tell me what I needed to do that was in the best interest for us all, that was according to His will. I was not led to the typical verses regarding divorce. I was led to Isaiah 30:19–21 (NIV),

> You will weep no more. How gracious he will be when you cry for help! As soon as he hears, he will answer you. Although the Lord gives you the bread of adversity and the water of affliction, your teachers will be hidden no more; with your own eyes you will see them. Whether you turn to the right or to the left, your ears will hear a voice behind you, saying, "This is the way; walk in it."

I knew at that moment it was ok to leave the marriage. It took several years to reach this conclusion, but I now had no doubts or second-guessing. After twenty-nine years of marriage, it was over. My attorney stated as we left the courtroom that it was time to celebrate! I did not celebrate. I did not rejoice. I grieved.

No marriage fails because of one person. No marriage succeeds because of one person. My biggest failing was in putting my girls ahead of their father. I justified this in my head by telling myself babies are helpless and grown men are not or that children with special needs require more attention than a husband. Nothing could be further from the truth. God created families and a certain order for them to succeed: God first, partner second, and children next.

I honestly knew that but couldn't or wouldn't do it. I think I even put my kids ahead of God at some point. I remember praying about that, asking God to change my heart and keep Him first, not my kids. Yes, I was the other side of the coin in our failed marriage.

Statistics at one time stated that when a disabled child is in the family, the divorce rates soar to 80 percent. This number has since been debunked but is still higher than the average American family divorce rate, which is already high enough to be upsetting. This is not to say that the disabled child is the cause of failed marriages, only that the family dynamic can create uneven workloads and added stressors. A single parent of a disabled child is likely reading this. I have great compassion for you. It is no easy task, but it can be done and done well with God's help.

My daughters agreed that Dad needed to leave, but even so, each of them had a difficult adjustment to the loss. My youngest, who was eight at the time, found an old T-shirt of her dad's and insisted on wearing it to bed every night. Of course I allowed this. She also began sleeping with me, which I also allowed. My oldest at twenty-two, Andrea, said she loved our home of girls only and it was much better this way; however, she needed counseling for some excessive OCD behaviors that immediately surfaced upon her dad's exit from the family.

My third daughter was eleven at the time and would ride her bike five miles to toss notes over the fence of the patio to her dad's apartment, begging him to call her and see her. Over time, she ultimately became suicidal. She began cutting, used drugs and alcohol, and became extremely angry. Rehab, Narcotics Anonymous, and counseling were in order. Finally my seventeen-year-old began sneaking out and going to parties I was unaware of.

I remember several times driving the streets of our community in tears, searching for her at one in the morning when she was missing from her bed. Of course I questioned myself as to whether divorce was a mistake or more detrimental to my daughters than keeping the marriage going as it was. Even though all the girls were saved at an incredibly young age and active in church, I learned that sin is like a pebble in a pond. The outward ripples affect everyone in its path.

Thankfully they all recovered and settled into what became our new normal. It has been over twenty years since our divorce, and occasionally they may see their dad. I have always encouraged a relationship between them and their dad and never denied any visitation. I think it may have been simply easier for him to separate completely from all of us. He certainly experienced a tremendous loss as well, and we each handle loss in our own way. Sadly the girls suffered abandonment issues because of this, and my youngest is still working through that after all these years. I must acknowledge that today he does not drink in front of his children. For that, I am grateful.

We all settled into this life and home full of girls. Sometimes it was like living in a dormitory, and it would get loud and crazy, but it was good and fun. Ray Romano said, "Having children is like living in a frat house—nobody sleeps, everything's broken, and there's a lot of throwing up." I agree.

But I was enjoying the relative peace we now had. I was enjoying being single and making all my own decisions, of having some sense of predictability in our lives again. I had no intention of remarrying, especially with a house full of girls. I had never really dated, as their dad was my first and only love.

And then as God would have it, I reconnected with a friend from my childhood neighborhood. I was only six years old when we met, and over thirty years had passed since I last saw him. We never had any interest in one another whatsoever. In fact, we weren't even friends. He was three years younger, and when you are sixteen and he is thirteen, well, he's just another kid in the neighborhood.

He had sent an email to my parents years earlier asking about me, and my mom had given me his information to get in touch again. I thought, *Why would I even want to do that?*

I tossed the slip of paper in a junk drawer and forgot about it. And then one day years later while cleaning that drawer out, that little paper fell to the floor faceup. At that point, I thought, *All right, I'll email him and see how he's doing, but especially how his older sister is doing. She had been my friend after all.* This began an online friendship that lasted over a year before I finally agreed to meet for coffee.

Mike was a single dad who had raised his two daughters completely alone. He won custody of them when they were young, and after getting to know him again, I could not believe how much we had in common. But above all, he knew and loved God, he had a huge and kind heart, he was a gentleman in every way, and he understood Andrea. It sometimes takes a huge amount of patience to converse with and spend large amounts of time with Andrea, but Mike would tease and banter with her the way my own dad used to do, and she loved this. He also took a fatherly interest in the whereabouts, report cards, and activities of my other daughters. And I, in turn, grew to love his warm and thoughtful daughters. So six years after my divorce, I agreed to marry him. Who would have thought?! I now have six daughters, four sons-in-law, and four grandchildren.

"May the Lord give you increase, you and your children! May you be blessed by the Lord, who made heaven and earth!" (Psalm 115:14–15 ESV).

Fertilizer

> And we know that all things work together
> for good to those who love God, to those
> who are the called according to His purpose.
> For whom He foreknew, He also predestined
> to be conformed to the image of His Son,
> that He might be the firstborn among many
> brethren.
>
> —Romans 8:28–29 (NKJV)

The best growth comes with some additional nourishment. Friends are an important part of that growth. A good and close friend, or any friend for that matter, can offer comfort and connection to the peer group. Unfortunately Andrea was never able to make friends within her age group. Even though she is outgoing and friendly, she can also be socially inappropriate, especially concerning spatial distance. She would often stand nose to nose with people and make them uncomfortable. I worked with her on this for years. We even did her eighth-grade science fair project on this, personal space, and although she understood the concept of it cognitively, she could never apply it in real-life situations. Of course she has a specific spatial integration learning disability, so learning the information and applying it will always be in conflict.

Still there is so much we can do to enhance and nourish the life of our disabled children. Any extracurricular activities that Andrea wanted to try, I would encourage her to go for it and never deny her. She took art classes and danced. She joined Girl Scouts as a Brownie and continued for several years until the troop dissolved when she was in late middle school. She was involved in church and a church group called Caravans. Later in high school, she joined Young Life and was able to go to church camps that she still talks about to this day as being some of the best times of her life.

She also wanted to try gymnastics! Now remember, this is the child who struggled to stay on her feet if you accidentally bumped into her. How in the world was she going to stay upright on a balance beam? How was she supposed to do uneven bars when she couldn't even support her weight by hanging from a single bar? I tried to discourage her. (I feared a serious injury.) Andrea is tall, so I explained that gymnastics is really for the smaller-statured girls, as their center of gravity is closer to the ground. I explained the great core strength needed to use the equipment in a gymnastics class. I talked and talked.

Andrea said, "Well, I still want to try."

Ugh, I thought, *Why did I name her Andrea again? Oh yeah, brave.*

She did complete the gymnastics class with no injury whatsoever. Normally, I would stay and observe these extracurricular activities, but I only stayed to watch once in the entire session. My heart couldn't take it. I'll admit that I was a helicopter mom at the playground, so to sit and watch this was not possible for me.

Even though she could not compete with the others in many of these enrichment activities, I encouraged her to compete only with herself and just have fun. That she did. Most of the teachers and leader volunteers were so kind and accommodating. There are so many people that I would love to personally thank for helping to grow Andrea, but hopefully I did this as we went along the way.

I learned something about Andrea, and the same applies to all children. I learned to never limit their challenges or protect them to a point where they are fearful of trying new things or skills beyond what we think their abilities are. I noticed that I was often amazed at how much Andrea would push herself when the bar was raised higher than I thought she could go.

So I allowed Andrea to cue me rather than the other way around. After the gymnastics encounter, I resolved that if she were not fearful of trying something new, even if I were cringing on the inside and fearful myself, I would encourage her to go for it.

In doing this and trying out new things, Andrea also learned to accept failure well. I never avoided calling it "failure" if she could not achieve something. Failure is a part of life for us all, and I did not want to protect her from that reality. I wanted her to grow resilient to it. I wanted her to realize it is an opportunity to try again or even move on and try something different. She was, and still is, able to shrug off the new things she tries but is unable to do or unable to do well. But she has no hesitancy in trying almost anything, and she has perseverance that often leaves me awed.

She wanted to learn to ride a two-wheeled bicycle when she was about eight years old. Her younger sister was riding through the cul-de-sac on hers, so Andrea wanted to join her. We started with training wheels, but I could see that this was not going to work as she rode the bike leaning on one side the entire time. So off came the training wheels, and for the next two years, I ran through the cul-de-sac holding onto the back of her bike and balancing it for her. I was getting discouraged and tired, but Andrea would not give up and asked to practice every day. We did.

After two and a half years, she took off. I wish there had been a camera rolling that day to record the look on her face of pure joy and victory when she saw me standing in the distance and realized she was riding that bike on her own. I am quite sure I had the same expression.

If you have other children, I'm sure you've observed that when our disabled child achieves the same thing our nondisabled child does, it comes with more intense joy. Not because we love them more in any way, but because we ourselves have invested so much more in the outcome.

Andrea learned to use the computer and befriended some of the staff at CBN in Virginia Beach. She would write to them, and they would kindly respond. She would send them little gifts, and they did the same. Andrea was obsessed with them and decided she wanted to move there and work there. Mind you, Andrea was earning $90 per week at this time, but money and how much of it is required to live and survive is a concept Andrea has not been able to grasp. Even so, she was relentless in pleading with me to take her there to visit her online friends.

Now I know this may sound like spoiling or overindulgence, but I agreed to take her across country to meet the few friends she had made at CBN. They were so gracious and kind. They met us in the lobby and gave us the grand tour of the studio, and we were able to watch a live recording of the *700 Club*. Andrea was so happy! But she was not satisfied. The next year, she again begged to go back. I explained that I couldn't afford to make cross-country trips like this and she would need to accept that and continue to visit her friends online.

The next year, she inherited a little money from my dad's passing and declared that she would just go herself. I said, "No way!" I explained why in a thousand different ways, but still she persisted. She even went online and found flights.

My friends, my other daughters, and my new husband encouraged me to let her go and try this. I remember thinking of the multitude of horrible outcomes this could have and continued to say no. Andrea would not give up. This is not typical for her, as I am normally able to explain something to her and she will accept my decision. She may have sensed my hesitancy this time, as I had so many people telling me not to hold her back. I was being influenced as well.

I finally relented and bought her a new suitcase and some new clothes. I packed them in sets so she could pull out one complete outfit a day. She was there for three days. I booked a flight that required her to change planes at a different airport, both going there and coming home. I made a reservation at the Founders Inn, which is adjacent to Regents University by CBN. It is a secure hotel with twenty-four-hour security. The hotel shuttle would pick her up at the airport and deliver her to the hotel. I called them ahead of her arrival and explained the situation. They assured me she would be well-cared for.

With great trepidation, I gave Andrea my credit card and put her on that flight. She was overjoyed! I was a wreck! We texted and called each other continuously for the next three days. I had rehearsed so many scenarios with her but felt I may have forgotten something that would put her life in danger. I mean, I was a wreck! I prayed continuously for her protection. I asked if it were hard finding her connecting flights.

She answered, "Mom, it's not hard. You just read your ticket, find the gate, and follow the signs."

The trip went off without a hitch, and she arrived home safely with a triple dose of confidence that she could accomplish anything. She had had lunch with her CBN friends, went shopping, had another lunch with a leader from her young life group who had moved to Virginia

Beach, found her way around town by bus, and took herself to the movies, mall, and out to dinners. She even ordered room service a few times. She had figured it all out. My mouth hung open. I had underestimated her at every level. This trip was several years ago, and she has not made another trip like that alone since and nor will she ever again if I have a say. I aged ten years in three days.

Through the years, Andrea continued to make friends with women who were much older than her and would often tell me, "I just want a friend that can go to the movies with me or to the mall or out to lunch." These wonderful and kind older women were there for Andrea, but not as a peer would be, and she understood that. She has several friends with mild disabilities, but their parents would not allow them to use the bus or be out in the community without another adult supervising. When we include them in our activities rather than enjoying the activity with Andrea, they cling to me. This defeats the purpose. The area of friendship has been the one gap in her life that we hope to fill once she is able to be in a good group home, hopefully soon.

Why a group home if she is so capable of so many things? She tends to forget the most common, everyday things. She once left the bathroom sink running with the stopper in and flooded the bathroom and entire hallway. Andrea has no concept of money or proper spending. She is unable to cook or use the stove unsupervised, only the microwave. Because of her spatial issues, she will stand too close to a flame or entirely forget to turn the stove or oven off. She is unable to cross a street without a traffic signal. Judging distance and the speed of oncoming cars is not possible for her. She still does not dress herself properly and will often button blouses off-kilter, leave her collar turned in or her pants inside her sock, put on mismatched socks, forget to comb her hair, and leave toothpaste on her face, as she rarely checks herself in the mirror, and when she does, she doesn't notice what is amiss.

This may be something that can be overlooked in the day to day, but not in the workplace and not in the world. She is also a very social being. She may be able to live alone, with support, but has stated she doesn't want to. She is looking forward to a group home setting and hopes it will be a place where they work together and have group recreation.

In many ways, I envy Andrea. She doesn't wear makeup and doesn't want to. She doesn't care about clothes, jewelry, or shoes. If it's comfortable, she is good to go. She has no concerns about her appearance or what other people think. I asked her once if I could pluck her eyebrows as this would really improve her overall appearance.

She looked horrified and said, "No, why would I ever do that?!"

I wish I were as free. Surely God doesn't care about these things, so why do we?

Surrounding Growth

> But you are a chosen generation, a royal
> priesthood, a holy nation, His own special
> people, that you may proclaim the praises of
> Him who called you out of darkness into His
> marvelous light.
>
> —1 Peter 2:9 (NKJV)

If you have other children, I am sure you've noticed the benefits of their sibling relationships and rivalries. It is no small task to teach your other children to have the patience and compassion required of their disabled sibling. Andrea is as imperfect as the rest of us. As a young child, she would instigate little wars amongst her siblings and then sit by and watch the outcome. She would talk incessantly to the point, where nobody else could get a word in. There were constant reminders about what an actual two-way conversation looked like and should be. It took Andrea decades to catch on, and her sisters would become frustrated and irritated by her.

On the other hand, when Andrea was going through a medical crisis of some kind or saw that she was being mistreated in anyway, they stepped up to the plate. It was most difficult at home. I recall a rude remark one of her sisters said, and Andrea was in tears.

I took that daughter aside and explained, "God could have chosen you to have Andrea's challenges, but He did not." I left her in her room to think about that.

As parents, we are concerned that because our disabled child requires so much hands-on work and interaction, we may be neglecting our other children or, at the very least, depriving them of the close relationships with us that they equally deserve to have. It is not easy or even possible to be 100% for each child.

I found myself often saying, "Right now, she needs my attention the most," "It all comes out even in the end," or "Life is not fair, and if you learn that now, it will be much easier to accept later." In all honesty, I had plenty of sleepless nights wondering who may have felt left out that day. I desperately wanted to spend more time with the other girls, but there are only twenty-four hours in each day.

We simply cannot be all things to all people. There were other times when a different child had the greatest needs, and at those times, they would get the most attention. Sometimes, especially as a single mom, it just felt like I was putting out fires all day long, pivoting on one foot to deal with the next situation.

One study done in 2013 revealed that children raised in the shadow of a sibling with significant health problems or disabilities may experience more behavioral and emotional problems. It states that, although the parents are equally concerned about their other children, the tasks associated with caring for a child with challenges can draw attention, energy, and resources away from the other children in the family. The study continues to state that there are financial, psychological, and emotional stressors in homes of disabled children that are simply not present in the same way in homes of healthy children.

But your family and mine are not studies, and families are as unique as fingerprints. The fact in common for all of us is that having a child with a disability powerfully affects everyone in the family. This, of course, includes the siblings. The effect is different for everyone and varies from person to person. There are common threads though. My daughters would become excited and happy when Andrea achieved a new goal or milestone. They really took pleasure in seeing her make progress. They also expressed feelings of resentment at times, as their needs were often put on hold for a more immediate need of Andrea's.

I think the most endearing memory I have was when Andrea was seven years old and had just had surgery to replace her eardrum. She was home, napping on the couch with her head bandaged all around. Joy, her four-year-old sister, sat on the floor staring at her for a long time. She then got her paper and crayons and worked on coloring a picture.

When Andrea woke up, she gave it to her and said, "I made this for you to feel better."

Joy also shadowed Andrea throughout the house during her recovery, helping her with the smallest of tasks, although many of these did not require anyone's help. Andrea loved this attention from Joy, and Joy clearly seemed to love giving it.

This may have been the start of my second daughter taking the role of the firstborn. If you have ever read the many books about birth order, they do suggest that when there is a firstborn disabled child in the family, the next child in line often assumes the role of the oldest. This is exactly what happened in our family, and with all the girls now adults, this role continues.

The girls were raised in a three-bedroom home, so none of them had their own room. As they grew up, some would get along better than others at different stages, so we often would change the arrangement. For a few years, it would be Andrea with Joy and the two younger ones together. Then there was Andrea with the youngest and the two middles together. It may have been easier for them if they had a place of their own to escape to, but this was the best we could do. I love what Kate Winslet said, "I finally moved out of my parents' house. It was only fair to let my sister have her own room."

I would like to say that Andrea and her sisters are close today and they all frequently communicate with one another. All her sisters have moved out and away, two are married, and the youngest recently graduated from college and is living about ninety minutes from us. The truth is none of them are particularly close to Andrea. I have no doubt that they would be there for her if needed, but it is not the relationship I had hoped for.

Again, Andrea can be extremely easy to love and relate to, but with her sisters, she herself is part of the friction and tends to revert to irritating behaviors of her childhood when she is around them. I have told her that if she treated her sisters the way she does other adults, they would see how wonderful she is to be around. I have told her sisters that if they take the time to get to know Andrea as an adult, they would see she is an interesting and fun person. To date, nobody has really invested the time to do that. In all fairness, they all have busy lives now and are building their own careers and families.

Now that they're grown and on their own, I asked her sisters, "In thinking back on what it was like growing up with Andrea, can you give me feedback on your perspective, what it was like for you?"

All three of them had overwhelmingly similar responses, "She was frustrating and funny."

"Frustrating in what way?" I asked.

"Mostly her incessant chatter and hoarding the bathroom."

I asked, "What was funny?"

"Nearly everything that came out of her mouth."

Hmmm, I'd call that a pretty nice balance.

Recently Andrea posted on Facebook, "I have never had a DUI. Are you able to share?"

I said, "Ummmm, Andrea, have you ever driven? Have you ever had a sip of alcohol? No? Ok then."

Or she will walk into a room and announce, "Mark my words!" and then proceed to give a diatribe about a government takeover of our lives or some other piece of news she's read and interpreted in her way.

Usually it leaves us all laughing uncontrollably, but she doesn't mind. She just walks away, shaking her head and reminding us to "mark her words"! Recently she saw on the news that our California governor was banning singing in churches because of the coronavirus.

Andrea announced, "There will no longer be sinning in church. You can do that after you leave."

Yes, she is entertaining. My dad used to visit and just say, "You know you could sell tickets."

I am profoundly grateful though that each of my daughters is highly compassionate and caring people. They care about the hurting, the disabled, the homeless, and the underprivileged and are involved in outreach to these groups. My youngest daughter has her bachelor's degree and is now considering getting her teaching credentials. My third daughter is back in school to become a special education teacher. My second daughter regularly fundraises for various causes. When she was a teenager, I came home from work one day to a living room filled with new toys. She had spent her entire part-time paycheck on toys to give away to Toys for Tots.

My third daughter and her husband had a homeless wedding. Yes, they met doing homeless ministry and decided to invite their many homeless friends to their wedding. They arranged with the church they attended to have them bussed from downtown to a park where the wedding took place. The bride and groom served sandwiches and wedding cake to their guests. Not very traditional, but one of the most moving weddings I have ever attended. In lieu of wedding gifts, they requested large print bibles and socks to distribute to their homeless guests. They were presenting an image of what it means to serve others and each other as a model of their marriage.

They have grown into kind and contributing members of society. I am certain that having Andrea as their sister has helped in enabling them to open their eyes and hearts to others' needs. They are all changing the world.

Dormancy

> But when you pray, go into your room, close the door and pray to your Father who is unseen. Then your Father, who sees what is done in secret, will reward you.
> —Matthew 6:6 (NIV)

During the years following college, Andrea's inability to secure a job of any kind, the absence of school and structure, was seriously causing her to regress behaviorally in many ways. She was also discouraged and spending more and more time in her room. What was she doing in there? She was praying, reading her Bible, writing in her journals, and listening to worship music. She was growing roots.

As her mom, of course I was praying too. "Lord, help her find a job close to home. Help her find friends and a connection in the world. Help her find her giftings." God promises that He gives spiritual gifts to each one of us.

> Now to each one the manifestation of the Spirit is given for the common good. To one there is given through the Spirit a message of wisdom, to another a message of knowledge by means of the same Spirit, to another miraculous powers, to another prophecy, to another distinguishing between spirits, to another speaking in different kinds of tongues, and to still another the interpretation of tongues. All these are the work of one and the same Spirit, and he distributes them to each one, just as he determines. (1 Corinthians 12:7–11 NIV)

He distributes them to each one. Andrea has a gift. What is it?

At this same time, Andrea's medical bills were piling up as she had no medical insurance and she was denied any SSI benefits. Following the divorce from her father, my attorney recommended another attorney who specialized in securing SSI benefits for clients like Andrea. I made an appointment and brought the required paperwork.

After reviewing her case, the attorney stated, "She will never get approved for SSI. She graduated from high school with a diploma (a stumbling block for her in the years that followed graduation). She tests with an average IQ, and she has no diagnosis."

I asked, "What do we do next?"

The attorney stated, "Andrea would just have to work like the rest of us."

I had heard about a job fair about sixteen miles from us. I could not get off work to take Andrea, so I printed up dozens of résumés and drove her there prior to the job fair date, pointing out the bus routes and numbers. I sent her off on her own, telling her to leave her résumé with every employer there. We again played mock interview, and I prayed. She made it to the job fair but then got lost in the area.

She told me afterward that an old couple asked if she were lost, and she told them she was. They drove her to the correct bus stop. God bless them! She made it home in one piece, but I had to remind her firmly that she was never to do that again. These were strangers, and I was horrified at the what-ifs that ran through my mind. But in Andrea's world, there are no strangers. This is very endearing but also terrifying.

At the job fair, a representative from a grocery store chain told Andrea to simply go into her local store with her résumé and ask for a job. She said she had done that, and they told her to do it again. So on her own, she went into the store, asked for the manager, handed him her résumé, and told him she had been to the job fair and was told to come in.

She was given an immediate interview in which she told them she would work any hours, any days, and do any job. She was hired on the spot and started working part time the following week as a courtesy clerk. The job involved bagging groceries, collecting, and corralling shopping carts from the parking lot and occasionally cleaning up spills within the store.

She was so proud of herself and her job! She would continue to wear her work uniform for the entire day she worked and proudly tell everyone where she worked. And work she did! She was always early, never late. She worked ridiculously hard trying to be the best bagger they ever had. I reminded her often that she wasn't working for the store really. She was working for God, and His approval was all that mattered. "Whatever you do, work at it with all your heart, as working for the Lord, not for men" (Colossians 3:23 NIV).

Once more, God answered our prayers, and what He provided in this job was above and beyond everything we had asked for again. The store was only one mile from home, and Andrea could easily take the bus or even walk. This business offered even their part-time workers medical insurance, provided they worked sixteen hours per week. They also provided paid vacations and even a pension to part-time employees if they stayed with the company long enough.

But again, Andrea's physical weakness hindered her

in the beginning. She could not lift cases of water like the other courtesy clerks; nor could she push multiple shopping carts as they were too heavy and too difficult to maneuver through the parking lot. Also her spatial issues created problems in trying to steer these carts without running them into the cars in the parking lot. The manager was gracious and accommodating and reduced the required cart number to only three for Andrea. This she could do. Even so, from the beginning of her employment to this very day, she will come home from her short workday and immediately take a nap. She is exhausted by it.

After several years, Andrea began to complain that the job was too hard physically. But I had observed that what she could not do in the beginning, she was now doing with ease. She now could lift the water cases and almost anything else that had to be lifted or carried for a customer. I reminded her that the physical aspect of this job was a bonus, not a curse. Because of her low muscle tone, it is extremely important for Andrea to continue to work her muscles all her life, but with no adaptive PE following graduation and no interest in going to a gym, how was she to do this? God knew, and He provided a job that involves all her muscles for three to four hours a day. I told her she was so blessed to be able to improve her health and strength and get paid for it! She agreed.

The other advantage to this job is that Andrea has gotten to know so many, many people in our community. It doesn't matter where we go together. Someone will approach her and say, "I know you! I see you at your job, and you're such a hard worker." Andrea loves this as she can strike up mini conversations with acquaintances wherever she goes.

Admittedly after doing this same job for fifteen-plus years, Andrea is getting tired of it. I see her at work, and she does not have the same joy and enthusiasm she had in the beginning. She is forty-one now, and yes, it is getting harder physically. My hope and prayer are that in the next couple of years or less, we will be able to find her new employment that is less strenuous or at least be able to get her total work hours reduced. I have every reason to believe that God will open the just-right door at the just-right time.

Meanwhile, I remind her to be grateful every day. She is now locked into an actual pension! It may only be about $100 per month when she reaches retirement age, but it is hers. She earned it, and it will help in the future.

The medical insurance provided by her employer was minimal, and still our medical bills were growing. I paid what I could monthly, but it was getting out of hand. So I went downtown and waited with Andrea almost four hours to apply for Medi-Cal.

The first question was, "Does she receive SSI?"

I said, "No, she does not. Isn't there another way to get some help with her medical needs?"

The representative asked, "Does she live at home?"

I answered, "Yes, she does."

"She could get it if she were homeless."

"What happens when a parent of a disabled person dies and can no longer support them?"

She simply shrugged. "Sorry."

Since Andrea was eighteen, I had been applying for SSI for her. Even though the attorney stated she would never get it, I knew she had to get it to have Medicare and a little financial assistance. Every application involved being evaluated by their own doctors and psychologists, and every application took months to review, ultimately resulting in a letter stamped "Denied." The reason given was, "We have found that Andrea is able to use one or both arms in a repetitive manner and is therefore employable."

I was outraged in the beginning and discouraged in the end. I appealed every denial, only to be denied again. I really did not understand the system or what they were looking for. I never wanted to prove that she was not employable. I want her to work. She needs to work. It is psychologically and physically good for her to work. The need was to supplement that work, as a full-time job did not seem possible for her and making enough money to meet her needs was just not happening.

I had friends tell me that Andrea needed to lose her job so the SSI review would go better for her. It would show she cannot work. But she can work. I did not want to be dishonest or deceptive in trying to get her some help. I did not want her seen as unemployable when I felt she was capable of many things. She just needed a little extra help.

I went back to the Department of Rehabilitation, and they suggested I go to Disability Help Center downtown. I took the day off work, took Andrea with me, and interviewed with one of their workers. I told her the whole story about being denied multiple times as well as Andrea's difficulties.

The worker excused herself to speak with an attorney, and when she returned, she stated, "We think we can help you!"

I was so grateful! The attorney filled out and filed all the necessary paperwork with SSI. The attorney had Andrea go to doctors for evaluations recommended by him. SSI had Andrea go to doctors for evaluations recommended by them. Watching this was like a game, each side trying to win their argument and prove their point. SSI was saying she did not qualify; the attorney was saying she did.

After everything was submitted and reviewed, again she was denied. The attorney encouraged us by saying he was appealing the denial and requesting a hearing before a judge. Well, this was new and a step further than we had ever gotten before. It took over two years before that hearing came to pass. The court system is not speedy. But we had waited this long, and God had been teaching us patience for many years, so we waited and prayed.

January 9, 2017, arrived. Andrea and I met with two of her attorneys prior to the hearing, and he prepped her as to how she was to respond. Here is the crux of it though. Andrea is incapable of being anything other than Andrea.

I wanted to tell them, "You're wasting your time. Andrea will always be honest. Andrea will always be herself. She cannot be anything else. Period."

Still they went through the motions with her, prompting her to respond certain ways to certain questions. They also told me that they were disappointed when they found out which judge we had been assigned. They said he was old and tough and he had denied many more cases than he approved, but he was also discerning.

I asked, "Could I go into the room with her?"

"No, you could not."

The attorneys said hearings took about an hour, so I watched as my daughter walked away from me with the two attorneys into the hearing room, and I sat in the waiting room praying and asking God that the judge be compassionate and able to see through all the reports to pure and simple truth.

Almost immediately after leaving, one of the attorneys returned and told me the judge asked for me to come in.

"Thank you, Lord!" I whispered.

The judge and a court reporter sat high above us, and Andrea, her attorneys, and I sat low, looking up at the judge. I felt like we were on trial. He began by asking us both to raise our right hands and be sworn in to tell the truth. Andrea raised her left hand, and I quietly cued her by tapping the elbow of her right hand. She raised her right hand and promised to tell the truth.

The judge then asked Andrea, "Do you work?"

Andrea answered, "Yes, I do."

"How many hours do you work? Is it hard?"

Andrea answered appropriately.

He then asked her, "How much money do you earn?"

Andrea got nervous and started tapping the table and shaking her leg. She did not answer right away but finally said, "Fifty dollars?"

The judge then asked me the same question, and I provided the correct amount of her weekly paycheck. He asked both Andrea and me if she were able to handle her own money. We both answered no.

His final question was really a statement to Andrea. He said, "Young lady, you should be proud of yourself for holding down a job all these years."

These questions took less than a minute, and the judge asked Andrea to leave the room and wait in the waiting room, which she did.

As soon as the door was closed, the judge looked at me and said, "I have reviewed the reports concerning your daughter, and having met her just now, I find that your daughter is 100 percent disabled and approved for SSDI, SSI, and Medicare, to begin immediately. I am disturbed that it took this long to grant her benefits and would like the attorney to make this retroactive for as far back as is legally possible."

I completely disintegrated in tears. I am choked up as I write this. It was such a victory for Andrea and her future. It was a nineteen-year pursuit finally achieved. I barely got out the words "thank you," and the judge stated we were dismissed.

As I was standing to leave, he said, "I hope my decision makes you and your daughter's lives a little easier."

The tough judge that the attorneys were disappointed in being assigned to proved to be compassionate, just, and caring far beyond what I had hoped for. He even had the consideration and insight to ask Andrea to leave the room before stating that he found her 100 percent disabled.

When we got back to the waiting room, the attorney looked at his watch and said to Andrea, "Well, that took all of eight minutes. You won, Andrea."

She saw my joy and the happy look on her attorney's faces, and she said, "Oh, ok," with a shrug. We all laughed.

I told Andrea we needed to celebrate and go out to lunch and thank God, as He is the one who made this happen. She agreed. We also both sent a thank-you card and handwritten note to that wonderful judge.

Had I known about the Disability Help Center years earlier, I would have gone obviously. If you are struggling to get your child or adult child approved for SSI benefits, then try to research an agency such as this. The Disability Help Center exists solely to ensure that eligible disabled individuals receive the benefits they are entitled to. They take no up-front fee but do take a percentage of your lump sum settlement, which they are well deserving of. It is a no-hassle aid in getting assistance and likely succeeding in securing the financial and medical benefits your child needs.

Fruit

> Every good gift and every perfect gift is
> from above, coming down from the Father
> of lights with whom there is no variation or
> shadow due to change.
>
> —James: 1:17 (ESV)

Our children are all uniquely gifted, and we need to keep our eyes wide open from birth. God does not leave voids. What a child may be missing in ability or skill, God will make up for in many other ways. Watch closely. I bet it was evident from birth.

Andrea was not born screaming or even complaining. She had a soft cry and then quietly went off to sleep. It was as if she were saying, "I'm here, but I don't intend to make a fuss or draw attention to myself." This attribute is still part of who she is. She is not demanding and doesn't seek or need lavish amounts of attention and praise.

When Andrea was young, I would have her and her sisters sit at the kitchen table and make a Christmas list of the toys and things they wished for during the holidays. It was the same year after year. The girls would ask for the latest doll or toy, a bike, or skates. Christmas is an exciting time for children. Andrea's list would be filled with names of family, neighbors, therapists, or teachers, and her request by each name of what she wanted to give them.

One year I told her, "These are great, but what do you want?"

She looked at me like it was a trick question. She had honestly not thought about it and didn't know what she wanted for herself. What she truly wanted was to give! I made a mental note of that and watered this God-given gift.

Even as a young child, when she would hear of somebody hurting or in the hospital or sick, she would think of a way to comfort them, give to them, and help them. This was inborn. I did not teach this! I am certain you have many stories about your own child and the many attributes God has given him to make up for any lack as the world may see it. I love hearing these stories because it affirms again and again that God makes no mistakes. He creates each one of us in His image, and just as we are, He brings His plans for our lives to pass.

Andrea was baptized as an infant in the Catholic church as a toddler, attended a nondenominational Christian church, and was raised in a Nazarene church. This tells you a bit about our progression spiritually. I have no personal criticism of any of these churches because they all helped lay a spiritual foundation that enabled me to seek and find the truth. I'm grateful for any church that teaches the truth of Jesus Christ. When Andrea was about three years old, we had neighbors who were members of The Way International. We became friends with them, and they were warm, loving, and caring people. I would hear them many nights in their home having prayer with a small group and singing worship songs. Two of the women would often stop by, and we would have coffee and discuss things of God.

They finally invited me to their small group and told me, "You know, Andrea can be healed and normal. The Bible says so." They then pointed out scripture that says exactly that.

I wish I'd have known enough then to have been able to look them in the eye and say, "No thanks. She's perfectly normal as she is," but instead I asked them, "What exactly do you believe?"

Almost every word out of their mouth was truth. But when I asked if they believed in the Trinity, they hemmed and hawed and ultimately said, "No, we do not."

This did not sit well with my spirit. They explained it away by saying the Bible does not use the word *Trinity*.

I agreed and reworded my question. "Then do you believe that one God exists as three persons: Father, Son, and Holy Spirit?"

Again, I did not get a straight answer. I still had not gone to their small group as something (the Holy Spirit) was holding me back. But it was a spiritual crossroads that kept me up at night and sent me to my Bible to highlight every verse from Genesis to Revelation stating that God is a triune being. There was no question in my mind that these people were missing that point.

I finally prayed the most simple and specific prayer I

had ever prayed, "Lord, if you want me to attend this group and be a part of them, let me know. I will do it. If not, then you need to show me in black and white because I will likely miss a subtle answer. Amen."

That was it! The very next morning, our newspaper arrived as usual, and the "currents" section, as it was called at the time, had a headline: THE WAY INTERNATIONAL. NEW CULT IN TOWN. I asked for a black-and-white answer and literally got it. You can't miss a bold headline! As always, Jesus was leading as a good shepherd does, with His clear and gentle nudges.

While Andrea was working at the grocery store, she was invited to a small local church, and there, the church members and pastors saw, acknowledged, and fed Andrea's gift of prayer. I am eternally grateful for them. The pastor's wife would often tell me that Andrea had prayed for something specifically for her that she could not possibly have known about, except through the Holy Spirit. Wait, prayer is not listed in the Bible as a spiritual gift, right?

Here is my belief. In all honesty, it is hard for many of us to pray. Most of us don't know where to begin or even know how we should be praying. I believe that anybody who can pray can only pray sincerely if the Holy Spirit is working in them.

In the same way, the Spirit helps us in our weakness. We do not know what we ought

> to pray, but the Spirit himself intercedes for
> us with groans that words cannot express.
> And he who searches our hearts knows
> the mind of the Spirit, because the Spirit
> intercedes for the saints in accordance with
> God's will. (Romans 8:26–27 NIV)

I cannot count the number of times I have passed by Andrea's room, heard worship music playing, and peeked in and saw her head bowed, hands folded, eyes closed, deep in prayer. I felt like I had stepped onto holy ground and quietly would close the door again so she could continue. Her faith is deep, childlike, and, above all, pure.

Her prayers are completely other-centered, and when she and I pray together, she never fails to remember everyone and every need she is aware of. She prays for everything! She prays for everybody! She prays for her church and pastors, Israel, the government, and the nation for healings and miracles. She does not quote scripture or pray in a flowery, churchy way. She prays from the heart. And then she calmly and assuredly believes she's done, that God has heard and He will answer. She never prays for herself unless prompted to.

I have often told her, "Andrea, we have that important meeting coming up, and you need to remember to pray for that too."

"Oh yeah," she will say, as if it's an afterthought, pure.

I tried to research just what this prayer gift really

is. I discovered the following: There is deep concern for people and places. There is compassion, knowledge, and a tendency to get lost in prayer. There is an automatic response when hearing of a problem, and that response is to pray. There is faith and a belief in miracles and healing. There is a knowing that if God heard it, He will do it. Often words will be said during prayer with information that you didn't even know. There is often a quick answer to your prayers, and you are honored when others ask for your prayers.

I concluded that even though prayer in so many words is not listed as a spiritual gift, there are multiple spiritual gifts required to pray in this way. So the gift of prayer is many gifts: Faith, miracles, word of knowledge, and compassion for others is the gift of mercy at work. And there He goes again, God faithfully giving Andrea above and beyond everything I could ask or think for her.

I certainly made my fair share of mistakes while growing Andrea, but the one thing I am sure I did right was to pray for her and her sisters every day and commit them to God. Other than that, it was all just, "I'm doing the best I can, and I trust God to redeem my mistakes."

It would bother me when Andrea would have a burst of progress or meet a difficult milestone and people would praise me for it. It was Andrea who did the hard work, and God produced the outcome, not me. So when I heard the song by Bette Midler, "Wind Beneath My Wings," I dedicated the words to Andrea. The lyrics were written by Jeff Silibar and Larry Henley. They are more than fitting.

Propagation

> But God chose the foolish things of the world to shame the wise; God chose the weak things of the world to shame the strong. God chose the lowly things of this world and the despised things-and the things that are not-to nullify the things that are.
>
> —1 Corinthians 1:27–28 (NIV)

In this short passage from the Bible, the words "God chose" are written three times. Your child was chosen by God, created exactly as God intended with giftings and abilities that will likely put the rest of us to shame.

> And I, when I came to you, brothers, I did not come proclaiming to you the testimony of God with lofty speech or wisdom. For I decided to know nothing among you except Jesus Christ and him crucified. And I was with you in weakness and in fear and much trembling, and my speech and my message were not in plausible words of wisdom, but in demonstration of the Spirit and of power, that your faith might not rest in the

wisdom of men but in the power of God. (1
Corinthians 2:1–5 ESV)

"On the contrary, the members of the body that seem
to be weaker are indispensable" (1 Corinthians 12:22 NIV).

I have heard many times that as we walk through this
life, we should keep one eye on earth and the other eye
on heaven. After all, we are created for heaven to be our
permanent home, not earth. I love author Max Lucado's
analogy of this. He says something like (paraphrasing from
memory),

> You can plop a fish on a tropical island beach,
> put him in fancy clothes and a comfy chair,
> give him a cool drink, and cover him in cash.
> He will still be gasping for air; his scales will
> be drying out. He will not be happy until you
> take him and toss him back into the ocean.
> He was created to be in the ocean, and this
> is his home.

In the same way, we were created to be at home in
heaven. Max Lucado also describes times in life where
we have true and utter joy but reminds us of how short-
lived and fleeting those moments are. We are not home.
We cannot and will not have that sustained joy until we
are. "No eye has seen, no ear has heard, no mind has
conceived what God has prepared for those who love him"
(1 Corinthians 2:9 NIV).

Do you ever think, "Why am I here? Do we live, die, and have it count for nothing?"

I think we all want to do something meaningful, something that will last, something that will leave the world better than it was before. I think all of us hope for more out of life than just working, acquiring things, and having fun. But in the same way that sin affects everyone in its path, kindness and love do as well. This is our meaningful work and the thing that will last into future generations and throughout eternity.

I love E. B. White's classic children's book, *Charlotte's Web.* When Wilbur asks Charlotte what her egg sack is, she answers that it is her "magnum opus." She goes on to explain that magnum opus means "great work." It may have been the *Mona Lisa* for da Vinci, but I believe our magnum opus is our children.

We will never know this side of heaven how our children have changed the world or the hearts and minds of men by their simple and sincere prayers and presence here. But the day is coming when we will see them in all their glory, the way God has viewed them all along, in perfection. "Then the eyes of the blind shall be opened, and the ears of the deaf unstopped; then shall the lame man leap like a deer, and the tongue of the mute sing for joy" (Isaiah 35:5–6).

Can you even imagine this? Whatever disability your child has now will be no more! 1 Corinthians 15 speaks of the new bodies that believers are given. They will be immortal and incorruptible, new, everlasting, and perfect.

When I began writing Andrea's story, it was suggested that talking too much about God would eliminate a lot of potential readers and I should minimize the references to Him. I considered that but realized, "How could I possibly write about Andrea without including God? They simply go together."

Besides, my intention in writing this was not necessarily to have a lot of readers, but to have the right ones. So if you are not a believer in Jesus Christ, I still hope that you've been able to glean some guidance in this book about how to help your child through the maze of agencies and likely hurts you will encounter. I hope you've been encouraged to keep at this great work that has been awarded to you and realize you are not alone. I hope you'll take the couple of seconds it takes to change your life and eternal destination. So simple really.

Just say, "I'm sorry for my sin. (We all sin). Please forgive me. (Only God can forgive.) I believe in Jesus Christ and accept him as Lord and Savior. Amen."

Even if you have doubts, even if you hesitate or feel foolish, step out and "just do it." Then watch what happens. You have nothing to lose and everything to gain. Why do this alone when the Creator of the universe is waiting and longing to help?

In the book of Mark, a father brings his son to Jesus for healing and says to him, "Lord, I believe. Help my unbelief." Jesus is pleased with his genuine prayer and heals his son. In a way, the father was saying, "My faith is far from perfect. I might not have enough faith. It's a wobbly faith, so help me to have enough." Done.

I remember the Jesus movement in the 1970s when I was a devoted Catholic. People walked up to me asking if I were born again. It was so offensive to me! I remember thinking, *None of your business. I'm good right where I am.*

I went to church with a friend of mine when I lived in South Carolina, and at the end of the service, the pastor approached me and asked the same question. I responded that I was fine and I was a believer.

He persisted, "But are you born again? You must be born again." This escalated until he finally said, "You must not leave here until you are born again."

I thought, *Really? Watch me.* And I left.

The words *born again* have been so overused that I think a lot of people don't even pause to give thought to what it means, let alone want to know. Jesus was never aggressive or pushy. Jesus attracted people by loving them, all of them, and people could sense that He loved being with them. Even little children wanted to be around him. He accepted and loved everyone, just the way they were.

But in the early 1980s while watching a Billy Graham event on TV, I thought, *Why not?* I prayed the simple prayer Billy Graham suggested and was done. I thought, *Ok, no harm, no foul.* I felt nothing different. But the words were said. The seal was given. I did read my Bible every day, even if only for a few minutes, and then went about my life, business as usual.

About a year later when I was at a party, I heard a joke that normally I would have found to be hilarious, but it was no longer funny to me. And other incidents happened that made me think, *How did I change? I did nothing to change. I made no effort at this.* He changed me. He still is changing me. He did the work. He always does. He always will. We are not called to fit into some church mold or work to become something we're not. He polishes and refines us in ways that we are not capable of on our own.

He created us to be unique beings, and He does not change our individuality. He amplifies it and perfects it. We cannot even begin to do this on our own, and we will never experience the great adventure that awaits us without Him. It is the same process with our children. May we each shine for Him as only we can do, in our one-of-a-kind way.

"Silly girl," the old lady smiled "your different was your beautiful all along" (Atticus).

Harvest

"Let us not become weary in doing good, for at the proper time we will reap a harvest if we do not give up."

—Galatians 6:9 (NIV)

As I was beginning to conclude Andrea's story, Regional Center has once again accepted Andrea as their client, and for the first time in her life, she has been given a diagnosis, ataxic cerebral palsy. Finally in writing from a medical doctor, a diagnosis.

The letter giving this diagnosis came in the mail last week, and I was overcome with emotion to know and have confirmed what my gut has told me all along. I felt like I was holding that coveted golden ticket that would open doors for services we have been searching, hoping, praying, and waiting for. Several days following this came another letter from the psychologist with Regional Center stating that Andrea qualified for their services based on intellectual disability.

Her IQ score had dropped significantly, enough to qualify for their services. Why? The psychologist explained IQ sometimes drops once school is no longer a part of their lives, and Andrea was not wearing hearing aids during the testing so her auditory memory score was not as high as it used to be. Hmmm, she reads constantly. She behaves no differently than she ever did.

None of this is relevant in defining Andrea. She is who she is. The importance of these diagnoses is that the doors will now open for her to move forward with assistance in finding more independence, a place to live, and different employment. I asked her primary doctor how it possibly could have taken forty years to diagnose her. Her doctor told me that they know much more now than they did forty years ago and the diagnostics are much more accurate now. I looked back, momentarily, and thought, *Wow, had she been given these labels from birth, so many services would have been available to her.* I looked further back and thought, *Wow, had she been born just one generation earlier, they might have put her in an institution.*

So instead of looking back at all, we are simply choosing gratitude. God has placed Andrea here in this generation. Esther 4:14 says, "Perhaps you were born for such a time as this." Consider that the Rehabilitation Act wasn't passed until 1973. It contained language that for the first time prohibited discrimination and created rights for disabled persons. Andrea was born only six years later. There have been a lot of positive changes in society since then, but we still have work to do. It is one thing to accept the disabled and make compensations for them. It is quite another to view them as valuable, worthy, and necessary.

Regional Center has since requested an MRI and genetic testing. The outcome of these tests is also irrelevant at this juncture. We recently met with a caseworker at Regional Center who developed a plan to prepare Andrea to find new employment, become more involved in community social events, meet others more like herself, and ultimately get her into an apartment with a roommate.

Looking back over the last two years, it is mind-blowing how forty years of prayers have been answered almost all at once, like a floodgate of blessings. In Biblestudy.org, it states that the number forty is used "146 times in Scripture and symbolizes a period of testing, trial or probation." God continues to prove that we can trust Him, that He has our absolute best interest in mind, and that He has and holds all the answers and will give them in His perfect time. "Therefore the Lord waits to be gracious to you, and therefore he exalts himself to show mercy to you. For the Lord is a God of justice; blessed are all those who wait for him" (Isaiah 30:18 ESV).

What if our prayers were not answered in the way we had hoped? What if again Andrea were denied any help or services? What if your child is denied everything you apply for and continually falls through the gap? I think God calls us to be steadfast under trial. He knows when and how to pour out blessings on you and your child in ways far better than what we could imagine.

But in my years of walking with Him, I have concluded one thing with certainty: If He said no to every prayer request and we were left with nothing more than a relationship with Him, it would be enough! His love endures forever! He has promised us a crown of life! Anything more is just icing on the cake and grace upon grace. He lavishes us with every good thing.

> Therefore, I tell you, do not be anxious about your life, what you will eat or what you will drink, nor about your body, what you will put on. Is not life more than food, and the body more than clothing? Look at the birds of the

air: they neither sow nor reap nor gather into barns, and yet your heavenly Father feeds them. Are you not of more value than they? And which of you by being anxious can add a single hour to his span of life? And why are you anxious about clothing? Consider the lilies of the field, how they grow: they neither toil nor spin, yet I tell you, even Solomon in all his glory was not arrayed like one of these. (Matthew 6:25–34 ESV)

This is a beautiful teaching from Jesus about why we should not worry, but let's be honest. These are our kids! We do worry, especially about their future without us once we are gone. I think that the more often we see (and remember) His hand in their lives and ours, we learn to let go of that worry, little by little. We learn to trust that He is the perfect Father and provider, not us.

When Andrea was sixteen months old, we took a trip to Seattle, Washington, to visit friends for a few days. While there, we were walking down a pier to see one of the ships docked there. My friend was wearing high heels and carrying Andrea, who still was not walking. Her heel got stuck in the crevice of the pier, and she began falling forward. I was behind her and could only see a fall coming that I could not stop, that would crush my baby.

Out of nowhere, a man stepped up, caught them both, and steadied my friend, and although later my friend discovered she had broken her ankle, not a hair of Andrea's head was harmed. We all looked around to thank that man, but there was no one on that long pier but us. My friend, her husband, myself, and my husband were all baffled that he was nowhere to be found.

This was an exceptionally long pier, and even if he had run after catching them, we would still see him somewhere along the pier. I believed then and believe today that God employed an angel to protect them both. "For he will command his angels concerning you to guard you in all your ways" (Psalm 91:11 NIV). He truly does "watch over our coming and going, both now and forevermore" (Psalm 121:8 NIV).

In 2017, Andrea was walking to her bus stop on her way to work, like she has been doing for years, when a pitbull/boxer mix, a loose dog, came out of nowhere and attacked her, leaving her with serious injuries. The damage was repaired with surgery in the emergency room, her mind was restored with counseling and God, and this traumatic event that seemed so horrible at that time resulted in a monetary settlement for Andrea that has been placed in a trust and will see her through for the rest of her life!

Gone are my worries about what is to become of her once I am gone. "As for you, you meant evil against me, but God used it for good in order to bring about this present result" (Genesis 50:20 NASB). We have all seen so many things come against our kids that seem evil or are just plain difficult and unfair. Sometimes they are evil. But God can turn it all to good.

He loves us! He always has! He always will! His love is constant and never changing! There is nothing we can do to make Him love us more! There is nothing we can do to make Him love us less! As my dear pastor used to say, "It's a parent thing."

CONCLUSION

He <u>found</u> him in a desert land, and in the
howling waste of the wilderness; he encircled
him, he cared for him, he kept him as the
apple of his eye.

—Deuteronomy 21:10 (ESV)

Today, Andrea is working with Regional Center and
their programs to prepare for a new job. She is back in
school at a community college and one class away from
receiving a certificate to be a preschool assistant. And as
we conclude this part of our journey, Andrea was recently
selected to rent in a special needs apartment complex,
newly built and unique in our area. The odds were one
in six thousand that she would be accepted here. The
facility is for county residents, and Andrea lives inside
the city boundaries. There are 309,000 disabled adults
in our county who would have priority placement, so
of course we were ecstatic. I called to confirm that this
letter was correct since the odds of her getting selected
for that apartment were so astronomical. And then about

a month later, I received a letter stating she had been denied after all.

Interestingly I didn't get upset or emotional about this disappointment. God immediately reminded me that He is simply working, as He has all along, in Andrea's best interest.

There are many times in the Bible when God said, "Go." He told Noah to *go* into the ark. He told Abram to *go* to a land He would show him. God told Moses to *go* and lead the Israelites out of Egypt. Jesus often said to *go*.

So it should not have surprised us when after so many years of waiting and praying, God told us to *go*. To leave the one place we called home for decades took an act of faith and obedience. But God confirmed again and again that we were doing the right thing.

We have been in our new home and new state for less than nine months. Andrea is now in Special Olympics, a new regional center, and a nonprofit organization where she goes four days a week for activities and life skills, and for the first time in her life, she has friendships and a peer group.

Last week we were told there is a room available for her with two other female clients where she will have round-the-clock supervision and assistance with cooking and staying organized and yet be allowed all the freedoms she is capable of and accustomed to. This is a beautiful home on a golf course in a gated community. Not only that, but Andrea will not be moving into a home with strangers. She knows these women from the program she has been attending during the day and is excited about the move. It sounds like a broken record to repeatedly state that God continues to exceed all our expectations, but then that is how much He loves His kids and exactly how He works.

Finding appropriate housing or homes for our disabled adult kids is not a simple or quick process. How do we even know where to start in meeting the many needs of our children? I always defer to "Your word is a lamp for my feet, a light on my path" (Psalm 119:105 NIV).

Every crossroads, decision, or choice we make can be directed by Him. We just have to ask, and without fail, the light shines on the direction we need to take. And since He desires the best for our children, we can trust where He leads. This journey we are all on is a laborious climb, not a sprint, but we have the wind at our back when we co-labor with God.

Martin Luther King Jr. had a dream for his four little children. And I have a dream for mine, that one day we will live in a world where the seemingly different are not ignored, debased, or dismissed, but seen as children of the living God with purpose, worth, and potential.

My hope and prayer are that when any of us encounter a different person, baby, child, or adult, we will see them as a masterpiece, a magnum opus, that we will see the possibilities in their lives and gifts to leave a mark and change the world.

They can.
They are.
And they will.
This is their divine destiny.
(And ours is to help them.)

CPSIA information can be obtained
at www.ICGtesting.com
Printed in the USA
FSHW011959270721
83618FS